52 Letters

A JERICHO WRITERS GUIDE

52 Letters

A year of advice on writing, editing, getting an agent, writing from the heart, the world's oldest book, marketing your work, battling copyeditors, the secret of style, probable vs plausible, what's up with Barnes & Noble, cannibalism, empathetic characters, writing phonetically and much more

love from,
Harry Bingham

Published by Jericho Writers Publishing, 2020
www.jerichowriters.com

Copyright © Harry Bingham, 2020
Print Edition
The moral right of the author has been asserted.

Copyeditor: Karen Atkinson
Formatting: BB eBooks
Cover design: Kelly Finnegan

All rights reserved. No part of this publication may be reproduced, stored in a retrieval system or transmitted, in any form or by any means without the prior written permission of the author, nor be otherwise circulated in any form of binding or cover other than that in which it is published and without a similar condition being imposed on the purchaser.

Praise for Harry's other titles

'Harry's style is relaxed and conversational, and you feel that you are in the company of a trusted friend showing you the way through how the book trade works.'

– *Michelle Moore, Amazon reviewer*

'Getting an agent and traditional publishing is one of the most bruising experiences you'll have in life, but with this book in your hand, you'll be facing it with a helpful and knowledgeable guide by your side.'

– *littlemisssunshine, Amazon reviewer*

'This book answers all those questions you always felt too daft asking. Bingham shares his twenty years of experience with the newbie author in a way that is easy to digest and practical to apply. He never shies away from the realities of the publishing industry, but that's refreshing rather than demoralising. And he manages to do all this with a good helping of humour, which makes what would otherwise be a pretty dry read, an engaging and enjoyable book.'

– *Alice, Amazon reviewer*

Contents

A word from Harry 1
The story you've left and the story you love 6
What Universal Workshop Style is – and why it's killing your book 12
Are Big Five publishers still the natural home for any ambitious novelist? 17
It's the simplest technique in fiction (and it always works) 22
How to self-edit your work without going crazy ... 30
More about editing: a follow-up to last week's email 36
Barnes & Nowhere 43
Crappy publishing outcomes, and how to avoid them 47
Crappy publishing II: the sequel 53
Giving thanks, and the power of detail 60
Openings, YouTube, and a Christmas cracker 64
Mindset mathematics 70
Feeling doomy? 76
The comfort again and again of writing something fictional down 80
A parcel of darlings 87
A faster horse 96

The taste of ash 99
Giants and gentlefolk.. 105
Hiccupy starts and some simple rules 112
Home baking and that all-important church fete .. 117
Do you write from the heart, Harry?..................... 124
Interesting. But why the cannibalism? 130
When supermarkets rule …..................................... 136
Pen-y-cwm – the end of the valley 144
How to write a scene 151
All about editing 159
A golden age... 168
The days that say no... 174
Let me count the ways 180
The secret of style 183
Late nights and leakages.. 191
Fractals, scenes and the bones of the fallen............. 197
New York gets Daunted 205
The power of the list... 212
How to title a book 218
Why bad reviews make me happy 224
Stick or twist? 230
The probable and the plausible 235
The internal and the external 240
I love deadlines 245
How to market yourself and your book –
in two words... 246
So wrong, it's right 251
Can writers learn? 258
The wriggle of life 264
The head in the bag 271

Oooh, tell me more 277
Swooping in, pulling out 283
Whitna raffle wur geen and gottin wursels
intae noo 292
What is this life if, full of care…............................299
A ginger biscuit and a nice cup of tea.....................303
Roasted chestnuts and a glass of mulled cider 307
The oldest book in the world.................................314
Afterword 319
Talking to Harry..323
About Harry Bingham 324
About Jericho Writers..325

A word from Harry

I'm Harry Bingham. I'm an author of a dozen or so novels, a few works of non-fiction, and a few other things too. I've been trad-published. I've self-published. I've had a ton of commercial and critical success.

Also: I'm the owner-founder of Jericho Writers, a company that does all sorts of terrific things for aspiring writers like you. Because of my long and deep involvement with aspiring writers, I probably know that group as well as anyone on the planet. In fact: delete 'probably'. I definitely know that group as well as anyone on the planet.

And every week, I write an email. That email goes out to our Jericho Writers list – currently about 40,000 people, but the total is rising fast.

Now, in the minds of the people who run our marketing, these emails are about selling stuff. They should be sell-sell-sell, with just enough useful content to keep people opening the damn things in the first place.

But the thing is: I'm a writer first and a businessman second. I don't really like selling stuff. On the other hand, I really do enjoy letting rip on anything to do with writing, publishing and getting readers.

So, in the end, we hit on a compromise that just possibly might be the oddest compromise in the history of email marketing.

The deal is this:

I get to write about whatever I feel like writing about, so long as the theme has to do with writing, publishing, agents, self-publishing, and all that malarkey. My emails can be insanely long – often a thousand words plus. Most of the time, those emails don't try to sell anything to anyone. I mostly don't even talk about all the great things that Jericho Writers does. I just talk about stuff that's interesting for me and useful to my reader.

That sounds like it might be fun, but a really terrible way to do business.

But the kicker is this: after my massively overlong email, there comes a list of PSs. The first one invites my readers to reply if they want. The last one urges my readers to unsubscribe. (I don't want to send emails to people who don't want to receive them.) In between those two PSs, if my marketing people want me to sell something, then, OK, I'll try to sell it.

And?

Well, I love writing those emails and people clearly enjoy receiving them. Every email I send gets a deluge of replies – and I always reply to the replies, so the conversation is two-way.

And, I've realised, there's a funny way in which people actually *need* those emails.

It's a hell of a lonely business being a writer. There's a lot of craft technique which is hard to come by – then illuminating when you have it. You can be wrestling all week with some manuscript problem, then find the clue to your conundrum in whatever I happen to witter on about on Friday.

I've wrestled all those craft monsters myself, and I've helped a bazillion writers do the same. That doesn't make me the Ultimate Novel-Writing Ninja, but I'm quite likely further ahead on that ever-winding road.

It's not just craft. There's a lot of stuff you just need to know about agents and publishers if you want to crack traditional publishing. If ever I want a tsunami of replies hitting my inbox, I only have to write about the difficulties of trad publishing. I'll get a heap of writers' stories, many of them quite moving to hear.

Self-publishing too – it's a game I take very seriously. Self-pub is simultaneously brilliant and terrifying. It's brilliant because clearly some people sell a hell of a lot of books, and it's terrifying because the techniques involved can seem daunting.

My aim is to blast through all your problems and keep your spirits up along the way. I'd love to tell you that this little collection of email-letters will give you a structured guide to writing and publishing, but it won't do that at all. What follows is a hotchpotch and a ragbag. It's a potpourri, crossed with a smorgasbord, and married off to an ill-assorted mishmash of patchwork salmagundis.

It's a chaos and a mess.

But I hope it's a fun mess. And instructive. And in a backwards sort of way, inspirational.

Because there's no particular order in what follows, it's a good book to pick up at random. The happenstance of what I'm talking about and what you're worrying about create, very often, a kind of golden synchronicity.

This book is made up of my first 52 emails, lightly doctored for flow.

To start with, my PSs were boringly functional, so I haven't included the early ones. As we've gone on, my PSs have become more baroque and exotic, so I've kept a few of them for flavour. Though this isn't a book which will try to sell you stuff, I've left some of the original references in for texture. Also, if you don't yet know Jericho Writers, you'll pick up a reasonable feel for what we do and how we do it.

And look: I said I'm not that great at selling stuff and I'm not. So – while you're still safely on the 'Look Inside' material, and before your finger has yet clicked that 'Buy It Now' button – let me tell you plainly: **these emails are free**. You can sign up to them at any time.

If you do that, you'll get a new email in your inbox every week – so, in a way, you don't need to buy this book at all. You'll have saved yourself $2.99 or whatever, and your life will burble forwards, hardly the worse for wear.

But if you have decided to join the conversation, then hooray. I like writers and I suspect we'll enjoy each other's company. Let's dive straight in.

I hope you enjoy the book.

Harry
Chipping Norton, Oxfordshire

[Editor's note: Throughout his letters, Harry mentions a number of links to things like editorial services, courses, formatters, articles and videos. We've added a full list of those links towards the end of this edition, should you need it.]

The story you've left and the story you love

So. Plotting. A Jericho Writers member brought me a plot problem, which we discussed as part of a recent webinar on plotting.

The issue was roughly this. The writer had written a long, long Young Adult (YA) book, then worked hard to shave 30,000 words from the text, without particularly altering content. (And that process, right there, is another subject I'd love to talk about one day. Reducing length without reducing content is probably the single most universal and effective tool in the whole self-editing arsenal. I love it.)

Anyway, this writer now has a 150,000-word manuscript, which is still very long for a YA work, although for epic fantasy it may be just about tenable.

Only then she meets an agent, and the agent says, 'You know what, I don't think this *is* Young Adult. I think it's a kids' book, and a kids' book needs to be well under the 100,000-word mark.'

The writer – battle-hardened and gritty – decides to slash one of the two storylines in her work. But there was so much beauty and colour in the storyline that had to go. The dragons! The castles! The caves and labyrinths!

The temptation, almost overwhelming, was to keep some of the material she'd loved from the now-deleted storyline.

Now, I've got a few thoughts about all of this. The first is that I *always* get the jitters when a writer starts making huge changes to a story on an agent's recommendation. 'You know, I think this would work so much better in first person.' Or: 'I really loved Jasmine, and I wondered whether you could give her her own storyline.' Or: 'I really loved this, but instead of setting this on the plutonium mines of Planet Trarg, maybe it would be more fun set in Renaissance Venice.'

(OK, I haven't heard an agent say the last of these things, but I've heard variants of the first two a million times over.)

The thing that worries me about these interchanges is that the agent has no skin in the game. They haven't always read the whole book and even if they have, *the writer is not a client*.

That matters. It matters a lot. If my agent (Bill) says something to me about a particular project, the accuracy of what he says matters. If I adjust my text to his specification, and then he doesn't like the resulting text, then he and I have a problem. Worst case scenario: he loses a profitable client, I lose an excellent agent.

Those possible consequences mean that when Bill and I discuss manuscripts or projects, we tease everything out. Pluses and minuses, risks and rewards. That doesn't mean we always figure everything out perfectly, but I can be damn sure that I'm getting best-of-Bill. An adviser to rely on.

When writers are talking to agents as non-clients, that relationship is just different. I've never heard of an agent being reckless or untruthful in those interchanges. They probably think they're being helpful.

But are they really taking the writer's perspective fully into account?

I'm not sure. If I were talking to the author of a 150,000-word YA fantasy and I had concerns about its age-definition, I'd want to explore both obvious possibilities. Is there a way to make the book emphatically YA? Or, if we chose to shorten the book into a proper kids' novel, then how could we best do that?

It's so damn easy for a no-skin-in-the-game agent to make a recommendation … and so damn laborious for the writer to execute it. So yes, *maybe*, deleting a storyline is the right thing to do.

Or maybe not.

But suggestions tossed out at a one-to-one session at our Festival of Writing in York, for example, are light years different from the conversations I have with my agent. They may be incredibly illuminating, or potentially wrong-headed and unhelpful.

So my advice to writers is:

I don't care that this person is an agent. That doesn't give them some golden halo of truth. It gives you a perspective to consider, and that's all. The right path is the one that you want to take, taking into account everything you know about the book, the market, and the opinion of intelligent third parties.

It so happens that this specific writer's question emerged from an author/agent conversation, but I hear the exact same things on the self-pub side as well. 'Oh, I saw this video which said that military science fiction is pretty much dead as a genre and Viking romance is showing near 50% sales expansion year-on-year, so …'

Again, that's an exaggeration, but you get my drift.

Don't let the data boss you. Don't let agents order you around. Don't even hand over your brain to a (probably superb) Jericho Writers editor.

This is your book, so own it.

OK, now that's a big point, and one I've wanted to yell from the rooftops for some time. But it's not quite the message I want to major on.

Because one thing I do see a lot is writers making big changes to their original draft … *but they haven't yet let go.*

The story that they've decided to leave behind still has this hold on their love and imaginations, like some long-gone teenage romance which still smells of ice cream and tastes of summer.

And that's OK. Loving your work? I'm all for that.

But when you leave a story behind, you have to leave it behind. You have to love the story that lies ahead, no matter what.

And if you are not truly in love with that future story – if you try to find that love and cannot do it – then that story is the wrong one for you. It will never work, I promise.

I know that (as ever) from experience.

The first draft of my third Fiona Griffiths book had this mad crazy over-the-top glorious ending. Just when you thought the book was just about over, there was another twenty thousand words of adventure. (Adventure that involved my character living in a tree trunk and eating sheep fodder. I did say it was over-the-top.)

I loved it. I really did. I still want to write a book that ends that way.

Only my editor and my agent both thought it was nonsense. They kind of regarded it as obvious that this was a little author's folly that would drop out in the editing.

Damn the pair of them, I realised they were probably right. So (sulky, still in love with the old ending) I hacked away at that ending and put something misshapen in its place. My editor calmly said: 'Well, that's a lot leaner, but you've cut way too much. There's no feeling left. You need to deliver a proper climax.'

So (damn the man a second time), I rebuilt the ending from scratch. *I fell in love with the story in its new shape.* I still had quite an unusual denouement, but one that fitted everything that had gone before. It just worked.

That book is still my favourite of the Fiona Griffiths books. It has the best ending of any of them but, until I found that place of love, it was in danger of having the very worst.

So these are the lessons.

Don't place too much weight on anything you hear from any third party. This is your book. You make the decisions about what to do.

And if you find yourself falling in love with the past, then allow yourself that pleasure. But look forwards too. Fall in love with the book you are making. You won't write a good one any other way.

Remember, if you want to opt out of these emails, you can easily do so And if you do that, these emails will stop, and your inbox will be a little drier, sadder and less fertile than it was.

Till next time, my friends, and happy writing.

Harry

What Universal Workshop Style is – and why it's killing your book

At our Festival recently, I ran a workshop on Gratuitous Sex & Violence. The class was super simple. We just read chunks of people's writing – on sex, violence, or both – and then we discussed them.

Obviously, it's often helpful if your work is being read out. You'll get useful advice just from that. But the real secret to a great class of that sort is finding issues that have universal resonance. Better still, you often uncover issues that aren't just little stylistic pointers, but things that overturn your whole view of a book. Tiny details that point to some much greater problem.

We had a few moments like that in the class. But there's one issue I particularly want to talk about today – I call it Universal Workshop Style, because it's so prevalent among writers who have engaged in a lot of university-style workshop sessions.

The passage we're going to talk about is one I've invented for the purposes of this email, but it's pretty close in flavour to the one we encountered in class. So let's say that our fictional thirty-something narrator is visiting his sixty-something mother in hospital, following a violent, but basically random, street crime.

That moment, written in Universal Workshop Style, might go something like this:

Bandaged and whitened by that hospital light, she lay there. I didn't speak, not to start with. One of her eyes was covered by a heavy dressing, quilted and somehow luxurious, like the duvet in some boutique hotel. There was one in France, a favourite of ours when I was still a young teenager, that had these huge cool rooms, heaped with pillows and endless quilts, and outside, a view of green lawns, purple shadows, and dim columns of cypresses.

Now pretty clearly, there's *something* good going on there.

You can pick out phrases you like: 'whitened by that hospital light' – that's nice, right?

You can probably also find phrases you don't like so much. All those green lawns and purple shadows – they're a bit much for me, at least in this context.

But the thing that really strikes you is the *writerliness* of it. The way a dressing is compared with a duvet, and not just any old duvet, but a specific type of duvet that lives in a boutique hotel. And not just any one boutique hotel, but a specific French one that the narrator (and his mother) used to visit.

In one way, the damn text looks bullet-proof. Fancy language? Yep. Clever imagery? Yep. Nice use of the narrator's inner world? Yep. The more of those university-style workshops you attend, the more your work tends to look like that. The more praise you get for writing in that way.

And look: that's not altogether a bad thing. Fine writing is nice. I take real care with my own prose style. I *like* pretty sentences.

But a nice prose style should only ever be at the service of your story and your characters – both of which university courses struggle to deal with. (How come? It's partly that you can only properly deal with story by reading and analysing a whole damn book, which calls for more resource than most university courses can offer. It's also, often, that the people teaching those courses are poets or slim-literary-novella-type writers, and that type of background doesn't necessarily give you a lot of storytelling heft.)

In any case, the big issue is this:

The problem with the passage we've just looked at – and it's a lethal problem – is that the pretty sentences just killed the story.

This guy is just seeing his injured mother in hospital, for Pete's sake! So we should have been thinking about the narrator, and what he felt about seeing his mother lying there. Instead, we went off down some spiralling cul-de-sac, to do with dressings, duvets, and the South of France. The emotional impact of the paragraph was entirely betrayed by an image that just took control and ran away.

Indeed, the passage would have been much better with a lot less fine writing. This chunk – plain as it is – would have been a huge improvement:

I entered the little room and saw my mother there, bruised and bandaged, still half-asleep. I was shocked. Upset, I suppose. I had never thought of my mother as old, even though we'd celebrated her sixtieth birthday two years before. And here she was. Looking old, looking frail.

There's not a single phrase you'd pick out there as being particularly writerly. Not a single image to harvest the praise of that theoretical university workshop.

But you are there in the moment with the narrator and his feelings. There's no confusion for the reader. No red herrings. No distractions. It's a much better passage ... and one much more likely to catch the eye of literary agents, or please an audience on Amazon, if you're self-publishing.

And if you simply have to have your fancy writing, then be my guest. Just stay with the character and stay with the story. Those things first, and everything else second.

So, for example, you might write this:

Bandaged and whitened by that hospital light, she lay there. I didn't speak, not to start with. One of her eyes was covered by a heavy dressing, quilted and somehow luxurious. But the skin around was purple and yellow, like garden plums. I felt angry, almost. I wanted the nurses to come with more white bandages, to sterilise the view. To hide it.

And then, ashamed of myself, I sat by my mother's bedside, held her hand and cried in silence.

That's nice enough writing, but you never lose the emotional thread. You have story. You have character. You have a book that draws you in, not spins you out.

That's all from me for now. More insights from the Festival next week.

Till soon.

Harry

Are Big Five publishers still the natural home for any ambitious novelist?

I mentioned last week that my emails were going to have a bit of a post-Festival feel, and this one is no exception.

So, on Sunday morning at the Festival, our opening session is always 'Futurecast': an attempt to look at what's been stirring in the industry and what all that might mean for writers. We have an audience vote before and after the session and try to see if any minds have been changed.

This year, our question was the one in this email's subject line:

Are Big Five publishers still the natural home for any ambitious novelist?

The audience split roughly 50/50 to start with. It split broadly the same way at the end. Our panellists split 50/50. The few people who changed their minds during the course of the session mostly went from YES to NO, but there were shifts in the other direction too.

All that – and I was never explicit about what I thought personally.

So let me tell you.

I think Big Five publishers are a great home for countless novelists of talent and ambition. That's been the case for ages now. It hasn't changed.

But *the* home? The *first-choice* option for *all* ambitious novelists?

That's what the question asked, and my answer to that is clearly, clearly, clearly NO. Here's why:

First, indie authors make more money.

There are any number of reasons why you might want to write books, and I'd never ever suggest that making money was the only sensible reason for doing so. But if you really want to become a professional author – one who makes their living substantially from writing – then you have to earn enough money to give up your day job.

And that can't just mean earning enough from one fat advance to tide you over for a year or two. It has to mean earning enough money with enough stability to allow you to make that shift.

And the fact is, indie authors make more money. If you look only at recent debut writers – that is, if you exclude the Lee Childs and John Grishams and J.K. Rowlings and other brand-name authors from the pre-e-book era – then there are way more indie authors earning a living from writing than there are trad authors in the same position.

It's not marginal, even. The gap is huge. (There was excellent data on this from the authorearnings.com website, but that wonderful venture eventually went to the great Trash Can in the Sky and nothing has filled it. But, for sure, the basic picture remains the same.)

And sure: there are plenty of indie authors who make mere pennies or, indeed, nothing at all. But then again, there are plenty of trad-orientated authors who try their luck with agents, get rejected, then give up. The result, in both camps, is to produce a very long tail of writers who make no money at all. No surprises there.

And how much money can you make from self-pub? Well, you might want to ask the noted indie, Mark Dawson. He recently shared data showing that he had earned over $750,000 from his writing.

Not bad, eh?

Only that's not an all-time figure. That's his figure for *January to August of 2018.* He'll crack the million-dollar ceiling before you've bought Aunt Betty's Christmas present.

Is he an ambitious novelist?

Yep, I'd say he was.

And would you say that his natural home was Big Five or self-pub?

Well, he tried both and he settled with self-pub. I don't think he made the wrong choice. It's crazy to think otherwise.

Second, literary authors don't need the Big Five anymore.

I said that there were authorial ambitions that have nothing to do with money – and writing great books is one of the very best motivations you can have.

And for me, as reader, the literary fiction I want to read is provocative, personal, quirky and unexpected. I want literary fiction that feels *awkward* in some way. Unsettling.

And, sure, the Big Five still produce plenty of really great books, but they're certainly not the only ones now doing that. Eimear McBride's *A Girl is a Half-formed Thing* was a blow-out, prize-winning success, first for Galley Beggar (who presented at our Festival last year) and then for Faber.

McBride too is unquestionably an ambitious author, but her ambitions were artistic, not monetary. Her book would never have been taken on by a risk-averse Big Five house. It was taken on by a tiny micro-publisher who believed 1,000,000% in the beauty and importance of what she'd written. When the book became too big for a tiny publisher to handle, it migrated to Faber, the best big literary house in the UK.

So for McBride, and plenty of authors like her, the natural starting point for a career may well be with a passionate and risk-taking micro-publisher. Those guys, penniless as they are, simply have more to offer a particular type of author.

But third, the Big Five still have a ton to offer.

Pointing out that the Big Five have their limitations is often seen as a kind of attack on them.

It's not. Plenty of authors should still aim at the Big Five. If you're a newbie writer writing (for example) commercial women's fiction, or mainstream crime/thriller, or book-club style contemporary fiction, or bookshop-friendly historical fiction, then the Big Five is an absolutely natural home for you.

Indeed, if you don't have a positive appetite to explore indie publishing, then I'd have to suggest that the traditional route is easily the best place to start out.

Truth is, it no longer makes sense to view these things in a binary way, because increasingly, authors are putting together their career in a mix'n'match, hybrid fashion.

To take my own career as an example, I've had some great experiences with traditional publishers, but I now make more of my money from self-publishing and love it. At the same time, my German publisher, for example, is just outstanding and there's no way I'd abandon that relationship either.

In short, ambitious authors of the future are likely to have portfolio careers.

They'll stitch their careers together around their own personalities, the projects that engage them, the opportunities that come their way, and much else. In my view, it is better to be an author today than ever before. There are more opportunities, more freedoms.

That's all from me.

Happy writing.

Harry

It's the simplest technique in fiction (and it always works)

Folks,

A short email this week, because:

(A) I am on holiday! And I never go on holiday! And I am not actually meant to be working! And there is actual sunshine outside my actual window!

(B) The technique I'm going to talk about is so damn obvious and so damn easy that when you get it, you get it. No complicated explanations required.

As with the last several emails, this one arose from a conversation I had with a writer at York. She'd just come out of her one-to-ones and I asked her how she'd got on. 'OK,' she said, 'but both agents told me they lacked engagement with the main character. They just didn't care enough about her struggles.'

Now, to be clear, the main reason for lack of engagement is NEVER that the character isn't nice, or cuddly, or loveable. Plenty of superb main characters are none of those things.

The primary reason for lack of engagement is simply this: you didn't get the reader sufficiently into your character's head, so the reader never quite made the emotional leap from real world to fictional world. There are lots of clever solutions to that problem, notably:

- Improving the inner worldliness of your main character.
- Improving the way you make the character specific rather than generic (so lots of specific memories, ways of talking, ways of observing etc).
- Improving your sense of place (because the more real your world is, the more real its characters will seem to be).

And so on.

Now, I may talk about some of those things in a future email, but for now I just want to talk about the easiest, simplest, and most enjoyable technique for increasing reader engagement.

It's very easy to do and it always works. It's simply this:

Make your main character really, really care.

I don't know what your character's specific goal is, but make it important *to your character*.

There's a whole mirror-neuron thing about fiction which means that if your main character is eating an orange, then it's kinda like your reader is eating an orange. Likewise, if your main character is in a place of danger, then so is your reader. But also: if your main character really, really cares about X, then your reader will too.

That's the technique. It's incredibly simple and incredibly powerful.

My work happens to be a great example, both of the problem and of the solution.

The problem is quite simply that I write crime fiction. My stories, typically, open with a murder and a police investigation grinding into gear. My main character is a detective and the investigation of serious crime is her day job. Likewise, my readers typically read plenty of crime fiction, so a little bit of murder is hardly unusual in their reading lives.

That could all add up to some rather drab fiction. 'What's this? Oh, sure, another corpse. Well, we had one last week, and one the week before, and dealing with corpses is what we do, so it's pretty much same-old, same-old. Anyone see anything good on TV last night?'

But what if – despite the environment, despite the relentlessness, despite the darkness – your character really, really LOVED murder investigations? Just loved them. Wasn't fully alive if she didn't have the smell of the chase in her nostrils?

You can already feel how that excitement could pass itself on to the reader. How the detective's joy in crime-solving could mirror-neuron itself over to the reader too.

And the technique is so easy to deliver. You write passages like the following. (This chunk, edited a bit for length, comes at the end of the first chapter of *The Deepest Grave*, the most recent book in my Fiona Griffiths crime series. Fiona's colleague, Jon, has just built a dinosaur out of office stationery and Fiona – characteristically – has demolished it for no particular reason.)

And that's how we are—me, Jon, the bones of the fallen—when Dennis Jackson comes in.

Dennis Jackson, my boss. The detective chief inspector who presides over our happy breed, this little world. A world that is, theoretically, devoted to the investigation and prosecution of major crime, except that the good citizens of Cardiff are too tame, too meek, too unimaginatively law-abiding to generate much crime worthy of the 'major' dignity. [HB note: see how she rejects ordinary crimes. She wants murder!]

[…]

Jackson fingers the wodge of paper on my desk. On the topmost sheet, there's a figure scrawled in blue biro, big fat digits thickened out by a lot of cross-hatching and multiple outlines. The figure is 453. On the sheet beneath, there's a similar figure, but in black biro, that says, '452'. And so on, all the way back to one that reads '19 December, 2014, Rhydwyn Lloyd, RIP.' Four hundred and fifty-three days since my last proper corpse. [HB note: ditto! She counts the days between 'proper' crimes. Who does that? As reader, you can already feel your mirror neurons starting to fire away here.]

Jackson says, 'You're still doing this? You had an attempted murder in Llanrumney just four weeks ago. Gary Whateverhisnameis.'

I shake my head at that. How does anyone think that 'attempted murder' counts the same as actual murder? They shouldn't even call it 'attempted': that's just a way to flatter failure. The crime is as close as you can get to the opposite of murder. And not just that, but bloody Gary Whateverhisnameis was stupid enough and drunk enough to pull a knife on someone in a pub where there were about twenty-five witnesses, and the entire investigation comprised little more than sitting Gary the Moron down in an interview room, telling him to make a full statement and then listening to his tedious, self-justifying repetitions as he confessed to the whole damn thing. […]

Jackson takes a bit of paper from the stack by the printer and fiddles around in my pen-holder mug, one that I was given by the office secret Santa in December. On one side the mug says 'grammar police' and on the other, 'warning. I am silently correcting your grammar.' When I was given the mug, it came with black insulating tape over the word 'silently'.

Jackson finds a biro and scribbles till the ink flows.

Then he takes my 453 page and throws it away. On a fresh sheet, he writes:

16 March, 2016

Gaynor Charteris

RIP

Places that where my 453 one previously lay.

I say, 'Gaynor Charteris. What, a coroner's inquest thing?'

That's not good English—my own internal grammar copper is already stripping down and refitting that sentence—but Jackson knows what I mean. I mean that any unexplained death needs to be examined by a coroner and plenty of those deaths require some form of police involvement, however sketchy. I don't count those things, however, and Jackson knows it. [HB note: She still wants a proper crime. That desire burns all through this passage.]

Jackson says, 'Yes, there will need to be a coroner's inquest, of course.'

'OK, let me guess. Some granny slipped on the stairs and we need to confirm there were no suspicious circumstances.' [HB note: This is Fiona preparing herself for bad news. She doesn't <u>want</u> the granny-slipping-on-stairs scenario.]

'Well, I don't yet know much about the incident, but I understand that, yes, there were some circumstances that do possibly seem suspicious.'

My face moves. An involuntary thing. I don't know what it says, what it signifies.

I just about manage to speak, though, and what I find myself saying is, 'Suspicious circumstances, sir? I mean, what? An open window, something missing, that kind of thing?' [HB note: same again. Her heart's desire is to find a case with a 'proper' murder. That desire is so strong, it's actually hard for her to speak normally.]

'Well, I don't know about the windows. That part hasn't been reported to me. But the uniformed officer currently attending the scene did say that this woman appears to have been beheaded. I daresay there'll need to be some further forensic work needed before we can be certain, but it appears that the weapon of choice was an antique broadsword. It's obviously early days, but I'm going to stick my neck out and say that no, Gaynor Charteris probably did not slip on any stairs. And I'd appreciate it, please, if—Jon, Fiona—the pair of you could act like a pair of grown-up, professional detectives and get your arses over to the scene without fucking anything up or making me want to strangle you.'

He hasn't even finished his speech, before I have my jacket on, bag over my shoulder, keys in my hand.

And off we go.

Yes, this is just another crime novel, launching yet another investigation, into yet another murder. But because the intensity of Fiona's longing is so strong, the reader is hooked into something similar themselves. So we go charging off to the scene of the crime already strongly feeling that this investigation is the most important thing in our lives right now. How lucky we are! Someone has been murdered! And the murder-method sounds gloriously interesting!

Unbelievably simple. And it always works. Yes: you need to avoid overdoing it. Yes: you need to stay consistent with your character. Yes: you need to write fluently enough that you draw the reader in rather than push them away.

But still. Simple. Powerful. And it always works.

That's all from me. I'm off to NOT DO ANY WORK. You guys have a happy time making your characters care.

Harry

How to self-edit your work without going crazy

A really common problem faced by late-stage writers is this:

> *I know third-party editing is really helpful, but it's also expensive, and I'm just not sure whether it's the right thing for me just now.*

You can add to that a whole bundle of other thoughts and feelings, along the following lines:

> *I'm going round in circles with this.*
>
> *I know the manuscript isn't right, but I'm doing a ton of work and getting nowhere.*
>
> *I know there's something good going on here, because I'm getting great comments from agents/beta-readers/my writing group, but no agent has yet wanted to take me on.*
>
> *I love this manuscript but at times I wonder if it's got any future at all.*

And so on.

And I guess the very first thing to say about this is – welcome to Planet Writer. I know a ton of pro authors. Some of them have had very successful careers indeed, but they face thoughts like this with pretty much every book they write. Those guys of course have agents and editors to talk to, so their angst takes a slightly different form, but the underlying concerns are very much the same. It's all just part of the writer's life.

So: what's to be done? The purpose of this email is to give you a kind of Angst-Reduction Plan … and a method for organising your self-editing work in a way that's simple, reliable and genuinely practical.

This email has a secondary purpose too, because it is, in effect, a list of all the steps to take *before* you decide to pay for third-party editorial advice. (And yes, we have a really great editorial service. That service gets consistently great results, but the aim of this email is to give you ways to *avoid* needing to get editorial help … or at the very least to make sure you get maximum value from the editorial process once you're ready to commit. My marketing people will probably kill me for writing this email, but hey, we all gotta die sometime.)

Sounds good? OK, so here's your action plan.

First, be clear about your goals.

That sounds so stupid and obvious, but it can be incredibly clarifying. Actually write down what you want. For example:

'I want to get this book published by a Big Five publisher.'

'I want this book to be the first in a successful, self-published SF series.'

Don't be embarrassed to think big. The purpose of this exercise is total honesty. If you want a six-figure advance from a massive publisher, then say so. Don't pretend to be all cutesey and modest. No one has to look at these goals apart from you. It's just a question of being blunt and honest with yourself.

Next, be clear about your fears or obstacles.

This typically will be a longer and messier list. Yours might look something like this:

'I don't get enough writing time in the week.'
'I'm embarrassed to commit to something that may never happen.'
'I hate my ending and I don't know what to do about it.'
'I didn't study English and I'm worried about my grammar.'

Or whatever else. There may be really stupid fears on that list, <u>*and that's OK*</u>. We all have some really stupid fears at times. Write them down.

And the act of writing matters a lot. You don't get clarity on what those anxieties are until you actually make a list. Writing is thinking – and you're a writer.

Divide your challenges into three buckets.

Some of your problems just are tangible in-the-world type issues, and they need tangible in-the-world type solutions.

So you don't get enough writing time? That's a real issue. You just need to make a plan that works. 'I'll find at least two hours a day at the weekend and find at least two hours elsewhere in the week.' Your answer will probably be imperfect, because life is imperfect, but at least you have a sort of plan. Those tangible problems/tangible solutions go into Bucket 1.

The next bucket – Bucket 2 – is just 'existential angst that I get because I'm a writer.' If it's vague and existential and not especially connected with problems-in-the-world or problems-in-the-manuscript, then it goes into Bucket 2.

My solution for those issues?

I don't have one. There isn't one. Welcome to Planet Writer. I never said this game was meant to be easy.

Bucket 3 is where you drop all the issues that are manuscript-related. Problems with your ending, your characters, your ideas, your prose. Big things, small things. Just write them all down. The more comprehensive your list, the better. Take a day or two to do this. You won't get it done in a session.

Organise your editing into layers.

I'm not going to tell you how to do that in this email. We've already created a great tool to help with that. It's the Self-Editing Pyramid, and it's incredibly helpful.

The big idea here is to organise your editing process into layers, working from large-scale structural issues down to sentence-level micro issues. That means that you don't find yourself wallpapering walls ... only to knock the damn wall down in your next stage of manuscript renovation.

Just move through those editing layers, one by one. Don't feel you have to write the perfect manuscript. Just try to get the best manuscript you can. Make your honest best efforts at each stage, but once you've completed a stage: move on. Don't rethink it. Momentum is (nearly always) more important than achieving perfection.

Set yourself goals and timelines and keep going. Just work your way through the edits.

(Oh, and if it's taking a long time? Don't beat yourself up about it. The editing process can easily take as long as the writing process. If it takes longer, that's absolutely fine. It's probably a good sign, in fact.)

(Oh, and if your manuscript still seems a bit rubbish when you're halfway through the process, don't worry. It's surprising how late in the day a manuscript can really come into focus. I remember doing a ton of work on my *This Thing of Darkness*, and really worrying that the manuscript just felt baggy and mediocre. Then – and this was the very final stage of my own editing process – I worked through the text, cut 8,000 words and got really precise about my timelines, places and all the rest. The bagginess just disappeared. The whole story felt sharp and alive. I now love that book – and so do readers.)

Phew!

When I started this email, I was hoping to cover the whole subject in a single email. But you know what? I'm over a thousand words in, and there's a lot more that I need to tell you.

So I'll shut up now and pick things up again next Friday.

It's chucking it down with rain right now. I've got friends coming for lunch. I've got a cold coming on. And I'd rather be writing a book.

Oh, well. Life first, writing second. Tis always the way.

See you soon.

Harry

[Editor's note: We have a variety of free tools and resources for writers, including our Self-Editing Pyramid tool. You can find a link to get your free downloads at the back of this edition.]

More about editing: a follow-up to last week's email

Last week I talked about the self-editing process and all the stuff you should do before thinking about getting third-party editorial assessment. If you want a quick recap of last week's email, then:

Figure out your goals. Be explicit.
Figure out your problems. Be explicit.
Tackle the real-world problems as best you can.
Accept the purely existential problems as part of your Writer's Journey.
Deal with the actual editorial problems, step by step, and layer by layer.

Once you've done all this work, you are at a decision-point. It probably doesn't make sense to do yet more editorial work. In most cases, the impulse to do that arises from anxiety rather than rational decision-making.

The traditionally focused author faces the following decision:

Get my work out to literary agents, or

Get third-party editorial help.

If in doubt, go for the first of those two options. It costs nothing to send your stuff out to agents. If they pick your work up, then great: it's good enough. If they don't, then great: you know you need that editorial help. You can spend the money with a clear conscience.

But you don't *have to* go out to agents. It's your call.

Plenty of writers know in their heart of hearts that their work isn't yet strong enough to be sold, in which case it's worth cutting out the rather bruising and unpleasant experience of the submission-and-rejection process. For those writers, jumping straight to an editorial process makes real sense: you'll get the feedback you need, and you'll get that in the context of a private, supportive and nicely human relationship.

Indie authors face the same kind of decision-point, except that there are no gatekeepers. If you want to publish, you can just go ahead and publish. If you have your cover all ready, you could, in theory, be published worldwide by this point tomorrow.

But the decision-point is still there, all the same – and it matters.

The simple, scary fact is that *the first book in your series is the most important book you ever write*. It's the entry point to everything else you ever do. This is the book that you'll be promoting via free downloads and Bookbub-style promos. This is the book that needs to turn the casual/curious reader into a committed superfan. If your Book #5 in the series is a bit of a dud, it's not the end of the world. If your Book #1 is weak, no one will ever read another.

In short:

You cannot let your first published book be anything other than stellar.

So you need to decide: Is this book good enough to compete with the best names in my genre? If you think the answer is no – and the answer is 99% likely 'no, not yet' – you should get editorial advice. If you don't build an incredible product to start with, all the marketing genius in the world won't be able to help.

OK, so.

You've ploughed through your self-editing action plan. Maybe you've decided you don't need editorial help. (In which case, fine. It's not compulsory.)

But maybe you've decided that, yes, you do need the help. Before you go ahead and send us your work, check that you've done everything you can at your end first. There's no point paying us to identify a problem you already know about.

When you're good to go, then you just check out your editing options and pick whatever's right for you. In most cases, you'll want the full manuscript assessment or the children's version of the same thing. (And, to be clear, though I'd love you to come to Jericho Writers, other options absolutely do exist. Feel free to check them out.)

Then comes the whole question of cost. And brace yourself:

Editing IS expensive. It's a skilled and time-consuming business. There's no getting round that fact. That's why you need to prepare properly on your side before doing anything else.

Once we have your manuscript, your editor will be hand-picked by our office team from our group of about sixty editors. We screen our guys very carefully before we take anyone on, and discard anyone who doesn't meet and maintain our standards. Your editor will typically be experienced in your genre and often have a particular interest in what you're writing about.

So what then?

Your editor will typically take three to four weeks to read, digest and take notes on your manuscript, before coming back to you with a long and detailed report.

That report, please note, will be totally skewed. It'll say upfront – but *briefly* – here's all the stuff you've done well. It'll then go into massive detail about all the things that aren't yet right and offer recommendations on how to fix them. A great long laundry list of problems ... with some possible solutions attached.

How you should respond:

At first – be ready for a shock.

Getting proper editorial feedback is an emotional process. I've been through it literally dozens of times with my own published work, and it's still emotional today. That part never changes.

So for twenty-four to forty-eight hours, you may well feel a little stunned, topped off with a little sense of 'how dare they!'

And that's OK. Go and kick some pillows or yell at the wind.

But as those first-view emotions cool off, you'll turn back to your editorial report. At a rough guess, you'll divide the comments up into the following chunks:

About 60% of the time, you'll think quite simply, 'Yes, this editor is right. They've identified the problem and the solution, and I just need to do the work.'

About 20% of the time, you'll think, 'Yes, I can see the issue, but I want to tackle it in a different way from what's being suggested here.'

About 20% of the time, you'll think, 'You know what? This is my book and I like it the way it is.'

And that's about right. Editorial feedback is *advice*; it's not a set of orders. If you choose to consider, then discard, some bits of that advice, that is your perfect right as an artist.

Your feelings at this point will typically have two components.

First, there'll be an undertow of disappointment. You wanted someone to say THIS BOOK IS GREAT. YOU ARE AWESOME. YOU NEED TO BE PUBLISHED NOW! And that's not reality. That's never how it is. But your feelings are primitive beasts and they'll let out a yell of two-year-old style despair.

At the same time, however, you'll have this strange sense of excitement and relief. The relief says, in effect, 'Yes! I've sort of known about these problems for ages, and they're a huge reason why this manuscript isn't yet doing what I want it to do. I feel unblocked and ready to go.' There's an incredible sense of energy release.

In short: you'll feel a little shell-shocked, but also motivated, powered-up and raring to go.

Now, I've tried pretty hard to keep these emails neutral.

On the one hand, I'm the boss of Jericho Writers and we make money from editorial services, so why wouldn't I pimp the product? On the other hand, I'm writing to you, writer-to-writer, and these emails aren't meant to sell anything.

So I'll finish up by telling you about my own personal relationship with editing.

Quite simply, I've always had a pro editor look at my work before it's gone public.

My dozen or so novels have _all_ been improved by that process. In some cases, that editorial feedback has made really radical, important step-changes in terms of quality. It's turned a mediocre book into an excellent one. In other cases, the improvements were more incremental, but still really important.

In absolutely no case did I think, 'You know what? I could have skipped the editing.'

With my non-fiction, my experience has been a bit more patchy. I can think of one book where the editor's influence was just malign. He made the book worse, forcing me to do stuff that I knew was harmful. (But he was a terrible editor, and the book was ineptly published.) In the other cases, definitely, my books improved, but I couldn't say that the difference in quality was all that huge.

Now it's true that as a trad-published author, I've not had to pay for this editorial input: I get it free as part of my publishing deal. But as I shift more of my work to the self-pub arena (more freedom, better paid), I'll definitely be coming to Jericho Writers for editorial help, just as if I were a regular client.

The simple fact is that an author's job is so huge and so up-close and involved, you do just need that professional, experienced, third-party eye to look over what you've done. Speaking personally, I doubt if I'll ever publish a novel without that support.

I hate editing, and I love it. And it makes my books better.

Till soon.

Harry

Barnes & Nowhere

A shortish email this week.

(And no, I'm not on holiday, but I've been wrestling with my wife's electric wheelchair and a new hoist we got for it this week. My verdict so far: mobility aids work extremely well in every way, so long as you are (a) strong, (b) fit, (c) mechanically adept, (d) have a complete spanner and socket set plus a full set of other tools, and (e) have all the time in the world. We've spent £1000 on mobility stuff this week and I've still been manually lifting a 55kg chair in and out of the back of our car. Brilliant, just brilliant.)

But: Barnes & Noble.

They've effectively put themselves up for sale, having made a loss of $125 million in the 2018 fiscal year. The company is making money at an operating profit level (ignoring deprecation charges) ... but it's still in a mess. And it's all very well to make money ignoring depreciation (i.e., an allowance for wear and tear), but wear and tear is a real thing. If you don't reinvest in your stores, they're going to look very tatty indeed.

Sales are still declining. If you look at sales on a like-for-like, store-for-store basis, they're also declining. That's not good.

So what next?

Well, I don't know, but it's one of the biggest questions in the industry now, as it has been for years already.

I seriously doubt if B&N will just go bankrupt, close everything, and never trade again. That's not on the cards. On the other hand, it still hasn't proved that the US market needs a large bricks-and-mortar chain bookseller. And it's one thing to put yourself up for sale: but who wants a loss-making firm built for a retail industry that belonged to decades past? That's not clear either.

My best guess would be that Barnes & Noble survives. It shrinks. It ditches some of its monster stores. It closes some unprofitable outlets. It doubles down on the good stores in good locations and works hard to please those customers.

That would be a good outcome.

But what if things go badly wrong, as they might? What if B&N is forced into a Chapter 11 bankruptcy? What if it is forced to trim right down to a mere rump of what it is now? And for all its problems, it still does $3.7 billion in sales, which still counts for a heck of a lot. This store *matters*.

Well, readers will be OK: they've got Amazon and a thriving independent bookstore sector.

Authors – you lot – will be OK too. We've got Amazon. We can reach readers easily. Indeed, the glory of self-publishing is that you can reach about 77% of the total market (for adult fiction) through Amazon and other e-tailers alone. At that point, why would you really care what happens to B&N?

But publishers?

Yikes. That's where things get really scary. Sure, publishers can sell to Walmart and the like, but is that really publishing? Or is that just shipping commodities to a store that would just as happily sell beans or camping stools or fish food or TVs?

If you ripped Barnes & Noble out of American retail, the publishing industry starts to look desperately weakened. Ten or twenty years ago, traditional publishing HAD TO exist, because there was nothing else to connect writers and readers. But now that Amazon is as mighty as it is, and Borders is dead, and Barnes & Noble is in the Emergency Room, the *necessity* of a large corporate publishing industry looks much weaker than ever before.

This isn't me predicting the End Times, because I don't think the most apocalyptic scenarios will happen.

But – we live in interesting times.

If you have an indie publishing focus, none of the Barnes & Noble news need worry you even a smidge. If you're trad-orientated – well, watch this space. The industry is changing. It may change the options open to you. It may affect the choices you make.

I know you just want to write books and not be bothered with all of this, but you aren't just an artist.

You are also a solo-preneur, and the industry climate will affect you too.

Thought-provoking, right? Just be happy you're a writer. We're gonna be OK.

Till soon.

Harry

Crappy publishing outcomes, and how to avoid them

One of the things about these regular emails is that I get regular responses. Sometimes you've got questions. Sometimes comments, or vigorous disagreements. And often enough I just hear about where you are in your writing/editing/publishing process.

And that's nice. I like that. And the news is often good. (Part of the secret of our success in helping clients is that we tend to attract darn good writers in the first place. That makes our job a *lot* easier.)

But also –

Far too often, still, I hear about publishing outcomes that are just awful. That we exist to protect you from. So here, as part of our Protect and Serve mission, is my quick guide on How To Not Get Published …

Austin Macbandits

Right up at the top of the list is Austin Macauley, the vanity publishing name that crops up most often in our postbag.

If you've been scammed by them, or if you're in their sights right now, I'll bet you have a gushing letter telling you that your book has been read with enthusiasm by the company's publishing board. The board will (I bet) have loved your book, but – sheez – the market is difficult, there's a lot of risk, and on this occasion the board is asking you to make an author's contribution of $X,000/£X,000. Yes, they'll put in plenty of money themselves. Yes, they'll offer you a full marketing package. Yes, if they don't publish the book, you'll get your money back again.

And if you find yourself in this position, please – just say no. Or, if your language is saltier, you might want to decorate your 'no' with a few well-chosen epithets taken from Anglo-Saxon and the Old High Dutch.

What Austin Macevil do isn't actually illegal, but it is, in my opinion, desperately misleading and utterly contrary to your interests. If you want to know whether they actually SELL books, then go into your local bookshop and ask to see a book by Austin Macawful. Or scan the bestseller lists on Amazon. Or just try to find any evidence of actual, real, honest-to-God publishing activity.

If you can't find it, that's because the firm is much, much better at taking money from authors than it is at taking money from readers.

The same, of course, goes for all those other scummy firms that operate in the same way. The vanity industry is now (thank the Lord) less prominent than it was, but it's still there. And it's still a pit of snakes.

Avoid.

The three-year wait

The next set of crappy outcomes arises not because anyone is evil, but almost from an excess of nice.

What happens here is that an agent or a publishing editor happens across a manuscript and gushes about it. That praise is genuine. They really mean it.

And then …?

Then nothing. Often, what happens is that an agent is very gushy at first, but as they re-read the book or share it with colleagues, they get cold feet. Or they start to work on some edits with you, then realise there's a lot more to be done than they first thought. Or they send the manuscript out to editors and realise that they have made a bad commercial judgement.

And that's OK. People get things wrong, and they can get things wrong without being either stupid or evil.

But agents and editors or anyone in that kind of position have a duty to you and your manuscript. If they realise their initial gush was over-the-top, they need to say so. If they don't want to continue representing you, they need to say so. If they come to think the manuscript is unsaleable, they need to say so.

And sure, you won't be thrilled to get that phone call, but your life will start again. You won't be in this eternal pause of slightly baffled hope.

That outcome can be avoided by you insisting, calmly and confidently, on maintaining an ordinary professional process.

Literary agents aren't *your* agents until you have a signed contract with them. If the agent wants to do some editorial work prior to signing that contract, then fine. But that editorial process needs to be time-limited and focused. If the process starts to feel wrong, it most likely *is* wrong. And, whether or not you are formally a client, if an agent stops responding to your emails or calls, that indicates that you do not meaningfully have a relationship with them.

If your sort-of relationship is with a publisher, not an agent, then exactly the same holds true. If it takes the agent/editor a few weeks to sort themselves out, that's OK. (The trad industry is never fast.) But I've heard of times where an editor has squatted on a book for more than a year, never really saying yes and never really saying no. And to be clear: that is not OK. That is not how real publishing works. You should not let that happen to you. Just move on.

The silent treatment

Another very common variation of the same basic thing is that an agent does take you on. Yay! You have a contract. Your book is going out on submission. But then updates get rarer and rarer. Your emails go unanswered. Voice mails are not returned.

What's happened?

What's happened is that the agent can't sell your book and doesn't want you as a client. What they ought to do is pick up the phone and tell you that. What they often do is just freeze you into non-existence. (Or a popular twist is that they spend six months giving you the silent treatment, then yell at you for harassing them and telling you that you're totally unprofessional and they can no longer work with you.)

And no. It's not you. It's them. Just move on.

And remember this:

We're here. We're on your side. We'll look after you.

If you're a member of Jericho Writers, or if you've come to our Festival, or if you have done editorial work with us, you're one of ours. You're on the team. You're a friend.

So if you have a question about the industry, or are concerned by an offer that's been put in front of you, then tell us about it. We'll give you honest, expert advice on what the situation is and what you ought to do about it. We won't charge you. There's no stupid hoop you have to jump through. Just tell us what's on your mind and we'll tell you, honestly, what we think you ought to do.

The truth is, writers who use us for their editorial work or sign up as members tend not to get into these pickles. That's because we know the trad industry very well indeed and we'll just keep you away from the bad 'uns. The bad outcomes tend to occur when people sign up with locally based and well-meaning editors, who just don't have the reach or experience that we do. Those guys are doing their honest best, I don't doubt that ... but their service stops at the factory gates. We try to make sure that our services last forever.

Till soon.

Harry

Crappy publishing II: the sequel

Well! I pretty much knew that my email from last week was going to cause some ripples, but I wasn't quite prepared for the tsunami that came back in reply. We had so many responses that I worked through the weekend and was still answering comments on Monday. Yea, verily, the walls of the internet bulged. The undersea cables were on fire.

This week, I'd been planning to write a 'Crappy Self-Publishing' email – a quick tour of the ways that self-pub ventures can most often go wrong. And, well, that email is still needed. I'll get to it somewhen.

But the volume of responses to last week's email deserves a proper set of comments.

First comment
I called it right. Dozens (hundreds?) of you wrote in to tell me about experiences you've had that accorded with the things I wrote about. Lots and lots of you mentioned bad experiences with Austin Macawful. Other vanity names came up too, but AM's is always the one we hear the most.

The gushy agent who falls silent: yes, plenty of you have been there too. The sad truth is that there is no meaningful external policing of either the agenting industry or the publishing one. We've found the Association of Authors Agents (UK) and the Association of Authors Representatives (US) to be ineffably feeble when it comes to clamping down on malpractice. They're not there to look after you. They're there to look after themselves. Sad.

It's the same thing with the vanity publishers. If the Publishers Associations in Britain and America took a hard line against vanity publishers, and if those guys were properly supported by the authors' associations and so on, the vanity world would find it hard to flourish. But … no one makes a stand. Indeed, there are still Big Five publishers who work with some of the most exploitative vanity publishers out there. Shame on them.

Result: the snakes continue to propagate. We make a noise. There are some great bloggers (notably David Gaughran) who do the same. But still the snakes seethe.

Sad.

Second comment

If you are looking for a publisher, and you are writing fiction or general-interest non-fiction, then your first best bet is to look for a literary agent.

If your book is not being taken on by agents, and assuming:

(a) You've approached enough agents (ten to fifteen)

(b) You've selected those agents intelligently (maybe using our very own AgentMatch)
(c) Your covering material is fine

Then your problem is 99% likely to be with the actual manuscript you are sending out. Sometimes that's because your writing just hasn't yet reached the right standard. Sometimes it's because you've just rushed to get the submission out there. Sometimes it's that your basic idea for the book is just too timid: that there's just not enough 'look at me' grabbiness for a debut novel.

But no matter what, if the issue lies with the book, you are usually better off fixing that issue (or writing a new book) than going to ever more marginal publishers and hoping that something great will happen. Obviously, we can help with editorial advice, should you decide you need it.

And to be clear, none of this is me saying I hate independent publishers – I don't and there are some bloody good ones out there – but it's a mixed bag. If a particular publisher looks or feels dubious, you should trust your instincts.

Remember, a bad publisher is likely to be much worse than no publisher. They can cause a lot of pain.

Third comment

Same thing with agents. There's a lot of unprofessionalism out there. Sometimes an agent can be just great with one set of clients, but still let others down.

But again: if a relationship feels to you like it's turning sour, then it has turned sour. Trust your instincts. I know it's hard to let go of an agent when it seems so damn hard to get one in the first place, but an agent who isn't working for you is an encumbrance, nothing more. Just let go.

Fourth comment

It's complicated!

The publishing landscape used to be pretty damn simple, and now it really isn't. So there's a huge range of publishers and sort-of publishers around today. You could line them up as follows:

- Big Five publishers (Penguin Random House and its peers).
- Major independents (Kensington, Bloomsbury, Faber, etc).
- Small and micro independents – thousands of them, mostly with a niche speciality.
- Digital-only publishers (Bookouture, for example, before it was bought by Hachette).
- Self-publishing services companies (e.g., Lulu, Matador).
- Self-publishing distributors (Smashwords, Draft2Digital).
- The service arms of big e-tailers (e.g., Amazon's CreateSpace service, now mostly replaced by KDP).

- Specific service providers (e.g., cover designers – or the magnificent editorial and copyediting services of Jericho Writers).
- Vanity publishers.

Many of these firms won't pay a dime in advances. Those digital-only publishers mostly don't, and some of them are outstanding.

Many of those firms will charge something: we do, for example. If you want our editorial services, you'll need to buy them. Nothing wrong with that.

So where's the dividing line? What's OK and what isn't? After all, you could perfectly well argue that the difference between a true vanity publisher and a self-publishing service provider is only a matter of degree.

And that's true. It is.

So let's say you are a retired midwife and you'd love to write a memoir of your service. _Good for you!_ What a brilliant project. You should definitely do it.

But you want to *write* the book. That part is your job. And yes, you want it nicely bound, you want it distributed on Amazon, and so on.

At the same time, however, you don't really want to be bothered with the proofreading, the cover design, the formatting, the metadata, the internal page layouts, and all the other million things involved in producing a decent quality book. Fair enough. That's totally your decision.

So you pay someone to take care of those things. Well, Lulu will do that for you. Or Matador. Or you could put together the relevant services yourself using a variety of specialist providers. Good! In your position, I'd do the same.

But the fact is, Austin Macauley will produce a book too. It'll create a cover. It'll upload it to Amazon.

So what's the difference?

The difference is one of honesty and approach. If you work with a decent services company, they'll tell you what they will do and what they won't do and what outcome you can expect. The conversation and approach will *feel* honest, because it *is* honest.

That retired midwife memoir *might* sell 500 copies ... if you have a strong local sales network and don't mind a bit of hustle. Will you make money? I doubt it. Will you feel proud as hell of your achievement? I damn well hope so! The achievement is in writing the thing, not selling the thing, and any family should regard a memoir of that kind as something to be treasured for centuries.

So a self-publishing company which lays that out clearly and upfront isn't doing anything wrong. You pay money to secure some services? Those things are delivered honestly and well? Fine. Great. I'm happy.

But a sleazy company that tells you how great your book is, how much the publishing board loved it, what the state of the market is in Australia/India/the Mid-West/Mars, how excited the marketing team will be to get the book – that's all horse★★★t. If it feels sleazy, it is sleazy. Avoid, avoid, avoid.

If you ever want to check the claims of those companies, go into a bookshop and see if the store stocks any books by that publisher. Ask the publisher for the titles of their five to ten top-selling books, then go and check out their bestseller ratings on Amazon.

If you just can't find any real commercial trace of those companies, that tells you everything you need to know. And don't be suckered by a tiny handful of successful titles. Any largish vanity publisher will have some successes, probably because the author worked damn hard to build sales. So explore. Look for titles mentioned on the publisher's website, then look at how those books are selling on Amazon.

It's a simple test, and it'll save you a mountain of grief.

Till soon.

Harry

Giving thanks, and the power of detail

Last week I told you I was going to do my best to write a short email this week. And well: mission accomplished.

My week has been thwacked by my little boy, Teddy, getting an infection that saw him being taken into hospital with suspected meningitis. The definitive way to test for meningitis is a lumbar puncture. That doesn't sound too great, and it really isn't. A doctor has to slip a largish needle between the vertebrae in the lower back in order to collect the fluid that surrounds the spinal cord.

This is a procedure where you really, really don't want the patient to be thrashing around, and Teddy (just three) was as good as gold. Two largish nurses stood ready to squash him if he started to wriggle, but he just clutched his monkey cuddle toy and didn't wriggle, didn't cry.

The test (phew!) came back negative, but his blood scores showed that his immune system was being pushed to the absolute max. So he's been on an IV antibiotic that the doctors cheerfully refer to as the 'Domestos of antibiotics'. (Domestos is a household bleach whose cheerful tagline is, 'Kills all known germs dead,' and yes, they do say 'kills dead'.)

Anyway, Teddy is on the mend. We've had two other kids poorly at the same time, and one very active five-year-old boy driving everyone else nuts.

So that's been my week.

And there's the bit about giving thanks. Something really bad could have happened to Teddy, but it didn't. Things like that put everything else into perspective.

(Someone should invent a festival around that whole giving thanks thing. Give me a few moments, and I'll come up with a name for it.)

But also: *detail*.

Writers often talk about people-watching, but it occurs to me that our observation needs to run much wider than that. If you want people to enter the world of your characters, the first thing that needs to happen is that they enter your world, period. You need to make your settings real, so that what unfolds on that stage feel compelling. So:

Teddy's cot was metal with very high bars at both ends.

It was painted in nursery colours – red, green and yellow – but felt cold to the touch.

A huge leatherette armchair by the cot unfolded to create a camp bed. You could feel every bar of that camp bed through the little mattress.

The blankets were thin, blue and somehow plasticky. They were slightly sticky to the touch.

In the night, nurses would enter silently to check Teddy's blood oxygen count. They saw I was awake, but they only smiled and said nothing. A red lamp lit up while the oxygen was being measured, and Teddy's hand shone translucent when it did.

At four-thirty in the morning of that first night, the consultant came in and said Teddy's lumbar puncture was clear. 'I thought you would want to know,' he said, and left.

Through a porthole in the door, I could see a paper giraffe munching paper leaves in the corridor beyond.

When I went for a pee in the night, I saw a mum and a dad in the parents' kitchen. They had mugs in their hands and looked serious.

And look:

You don't always need all the detail you come up with. You can write five sentences and delete four. Or write five sentences and smish together the two best half-sentences you create.

And you don't need all your descriptive stuff in a chunk. You can split it up and toss it out, bit by bit, through your scene or chapter.

All that stuff about descriptive writing being the part that people skip: it's rubbish.

Sure, no one wants to read three-paragraph blocks of description, but that's not how you ought to deliver it. Let story and character dictate what you do when, but you don't have a story worth telling unless it's set in a world that feels solid.

This email splits into roughly two parts. The first part told you what actually happened in my life this week. The second part told you what that world actually felt like. You needed the first part to engage you. You needed the second part to make it feel real.

Books are like that too, except they don't divide those things into two parts.

That's mostly it from me. Take a look in the PSs for the best Black Friday offer you're going to get this millennium.

And – let's be thankful, for mercies big and small.

Till soon.

Harry

[Editor's note: At about this point, Harry's PSs became slightly more interesting. In what follows, we'll give you some edited snippets from them, just to give you the flavour. Needless to say, any references to live events are now long stale.]

PS: Got something to tell me? Then hit reply. I'm massively behind with absolutely everything at the moment, however, so I'm not guaranteeing a prompt response.

PPS: If you hate these emails, if you no longer want to be a writer, if you are currently inventing an antibiotic so powerful it'll curl your toenails and singe your eyebrows, then you can unsubscribe.

Openings, YouTube, and a Christmas cracker

I want to talk about openings today, and so we will.

But first – ta-daa! – we've just launched our very own YouTube channel. Just six videos up there at the moment, but we've got a pocketful of others to release soon, so we'll soon have a proper little collection ready. It's been a lot of fun putting these together, and we have some entertaining ideas for after Christmas too. Do, please, explore anything there that takes your fancy.

Righty-ho.

Openings.

One good question I had recently was from a writer whose book opened with somebody trying to kill the protagonist. I'm generally in favour of holding back on the action early on. I want the opening of a book to tease me, not just burn me up in an all-action fireball.

But – aren't there genres where the someone-tries-to-kill-someone opening is exactly right? Like, precisely what the market is after?

And yes. The answer is yes. But you can still leak things out. So let's say you are writing some kind of alternative-reality comedy-thriller, where a waiter-robot with a grudge is trying to laser your protagonist's head off. Yes, you might have exactly that opening. But even as you're tipping over bar-stools and feeling the burn of laser fire above your head, you can tease some other mystery. For example:

All this was really annoying. I mean, robots will be robots, I get that, but I had a message to deliver and none of this was making that task any easier ...

That kind of approach allows you tease a mystery, while in the middle of a laser fight with discontented robots. I know *I'd* read on under those circumstances.

But my other big message on openings is to look after the reader.

The opening of a book is the most precious and most easily broken part of it. If you have a dodgy chapter 27 in the middle of your book, you should have built up enough trust with the reader that they'll continue to read almost no matter what.

Openings aren't like that. For one thing, people may read your opening – online or in a bookshop – before they've even read the book. But also, openings are more complex bits of equipment than other parts of your book. They have to:

- Offer the scent of story – enough to drive the reader onwards through your text.
- Set your characters in motion – and your characters have to convince and intrigue the readers from page 1.

- Start to open up your world – the physical settings and any 'rules of the game' that will apply through the course of the book.

Those are big asks. It's easy creating character intrigue when the reader already mostly knows the character. 'Oh no. Darcy is asking Lizzy Bennet to marry him – and we know she despises him – so just how badly is this going to turn out?'

It's a damn sight harder getting that level of engagement when we know damn all about the characters. The same thing when it comes to pushing along your story or opening up important aspects of your world.

The fact is that a reader has to *work hardest* during your opening chapters, because they have so much data to assimilate. That hard work is the main reason why readers may just turn off from your book completely – not buying it, or not reading it having bought it.

Knowing this, a lot of writers are lured into taking one of two paths.

Either, they decide that their actual opening doesn't have quite enough whizz-bangs in it, so they throw in a prologue (normally a flashforward to a more exciting part of the story to come).

Or, they decide that for readers to understand (say) the relationship between characters X and Y, they need to understand the backstory between those two people when they met as students.

Indeed, some writers decide to take both paths at once. The result can be a complete tangle. We sometimes see stories that start like this:

- Prologue: flashforward to an all-action part of the story.
- True opening chapter (character X's viewpoint).
- Second chapter (character Y's viewpoint).
- Third chapter (backstory about when X & Y were at college together).

And wow! That's four completely different openings. This book has just started four times over. However great your stories and your characters, you are asking your reader to do the hard work of beginning four times in one book.

That's a killer. I mean, if I thought about it, I could probably think of novels that do something like this and achieve a great result, but it's hard to do – and in most cases, it's simply the wrong strategy.

So as well as all the other jobs your opening has to perform, I'm going to add this:

- Don't overwhelm the reader.

Just keep an eye on how many characters (and names) you are introducing. How many timelines. How many jump-cuts. How many point-of-view characters.

It's not like there are actual rules on this. There's nothing that says, 'You may not introduce more than

X different timelines in the first 3,000 words.' But – the absence of fixed rules doesn't mean you can just do whatever the heck you like.

Take care of your reader. That reader is your friend.

That's all from me.

Except, oh yes, you've got to have this: the best writing-related joke of the festive season so far.

> *Q: What's the correct name for Santa's Little Helpers?*
> *A: Subordinate clauses.*

If you want a Fiona-Griffiths-themed Xmas joke, you can get it in the PSs below. (Fiona G is my detective character – and the joke gives you a bit of a flavour of her.)

Happy tinsel and glittery things to one and all.

Harry

PS: I'm human. This is an email. You know the drill.

PPS: Hate these emails? Don't want to be a writer? Want to knit socks and shout at the TV for the Rest Of Your Life? Then unsubscribe.

PPPS: That Fiona Griffiths Christmas story goes like this. The narrator is, of course, the one and only Fiona G:

> *I'm up in the Beacons. A cold wind down from Talybont. Coat, scarf, boots, hat, but I'm still cold.*

I'm with Bev. She's cold too. Cheeks pink and baby-fresh. Eyes streaming a bit. We've got evidence bags with us. A basic forensic collection kit, but what we've got in front of us goes way beyond any of that.

A long, long way.

Light glitters from the water. Silver, black and the palest green-gold.

I say, 'Mass grave, Bev. Awful.'

'Fi—'

'There must be, what, five hundred corpses? Probably more.'

'Fiona—'

'Just think of them, though. The victims. All killed the same way. And yes, OK, they were only snowmen, but snowmen with families. With friends. With snowpeople who loved them.'

Bev grabs my arm and pulls me gently away. Her eyes are bigger than Bambi's. Her cheeks are porcelain, rain-polished.

'Fiona,' she says again. 'It's a pond. It's just a pond.'

Arm in arm, we walk together down the hill and into all the joys of Christmas.

Mindset mathematics

It's the New Year. The mince pies have been gobbled, the reindeer stuffed, the tinsel-only party dresses put away in a crackle of static.

And –

A new year looms. What are you going to do with it?

That is, I know, a question for many of you: December is always our quietest month, January always our busiest. And one of the issues that comes up time and time again is the bulk of work to be done against the shortage of time in which to do it.

That problem is worse when writing isn't your full-time job, and it gets really serious when you don't have a book deal or self-publishing income to justify your labours to your family. The hours just feel too few, the works just feels too much.

And yep, I know all about it. Good writing needs a quality of descent. You lower yourself from this (bland, pointless, uninteresting) Real World into the beautiful world of your own creation. The deeper you descend, the more fully present you are, the better you write. That immersive writing infects the reader. If you're fully present in your world, the reader is likely to be too.

But the descent takes time. Finding the right route out of your current plot predicament takes time. Everything takes time.

So I know plenty of writers who measure their plans out in years. 'This year I want to really nail the first draft of the manuscript. Then I'll get a big edit in autumn/winter, maybe take a course, then aim to have the book out with agents by September next year.' Or whatever.

And, look, this is your life and I don't know your specific circumstances. So maybe that kind of planning makes sense.

But I will say this.

If you feel things are going slow, or if you worry you are being unproductive, then you can speed up. Indeed, you may be able to speed up massively. It won't even be hard.

That old saw about work always expanding to fill the time available is particularly true of writing, and doubly true of writing without hard external deadlines. If you think, 'September next year', you don't have a chance of completing your work before September next year. If you think 'September next year … probably', then you won't be done two Christmases from now.

So work the other way round. Give yourself a tough deadline, then meet it.

'I want my work to be with agents this year, which means, I want an editorial critique commissioned by September, which means I need a first draft done by June, so I can have the summer to think about it and edit it, so I need to write X words per month between now and then.'

That's doable. It always is.

I used to be a fairly slow writer. Then I got a pair of twins. Then, less than two years later, I got a second set of twins. My time available for writing probably halved or worse.

My book deadlines didn't change an iota. But I never missed a deadline and the quality of my work, if anything, improved.

All that happened was I changed my mindset. Before, I'd happily spend an hour lowering myself into my work. I didn't really expect to write anything useful in that hour. When babies came along, that just had to change, so it did. There was no big wrench involved. I just wrote differently. It was absolutely fine.

There's another kind of energy-drain around writing. If you have a messy situation with a publisher, with an agent, with a writing group, with your own adventures in self-pub, those things can prey on you. Energy that should be going into your writing just gets caught up in those messes.

And – well, I've been there too. I've had messy situations with plenty of publishers and they are draining. It's really hard to put your best work on a page if you think the book you write will end up being mismarketed (or, indeed, not really marketed at all).

But still. Getting yourself in knots about a problem doesn't solve that problem. You need to make bold, clear decisions about what to do. Then do it. And meantime, keep writing that damn book.

Here are the things that count as work:

1. Writing a book.
2. Editing a book.
3. Taking rational steps to publish your book.
4. Taking rational steps to self-publish and market your book.
5. Collecting the email addresses of your readers (which is really just a very important subset of 4).

That's it. That's all.

And work means actually doing those things. Not thinking about them, but doing them. The biggest secret to being efficient about those things is simply: deciding to be efficient. It's choosing to change your mindset, and building new habits accordingly.

That, honestly, is the biggest single change you can make.

The second biggest gift you can give yourself is simply this: don't ever let yourself get stuck for lack of guidance. So many people do, and it's just crazy.

If you need help in navigating the path to trad publication, then get that help. You're not an expert here. Why would you be? Why should you be?

You don't win points for figuring things out yourself from scratch. You win points for getting a book deal. So get help. Get rigorous, structured help of the sort that just takes uncertainty off the table.

Same thing with self-publishing, only even more so. Self-publishing is no longer a make-it-up-as-you-go-along game. It's a game whose rules have been pretty well established – at any rate when it comes to the foundational stuff. (There's much more room for variety when it comes to the more advanced techniques.) So learn what you're doing. Then do it. Biff-bam. It's a sequence of largely mechanical steps that you just need to follow.

Same thing with writing. If you have got stuck somewhere in your book, you are not the first person in the world to get stuck like that. You don't win points for solving your problems via years of tears and effort. You win points for writing a wonderful book. If the decisive action is to take a course or get an edit, you should do that. Your book will get better and you will get better as a writer.

It's as though there's something cool (in a holes-in-the-pullover, earnest-young-man-with-glasses way) about writerly angst. 'Oh, I haven't been able to write for three months, because I'm recalibrating my relationship with the letter R.' It's like the more angsty you are, the more writerly you are.

And that is horse manure, of course. Steaming and stupid.

You want a measure of being a writer? It's how many books you write and publish.

You want to recalibrate your relationship with the letter R? OK, be my guest, buddy, but that's on your time, not mine. It doesn't count as work. Only work counts as work. (And you want a reminder of how we're defining work? It's the list of five points above, the one that starts with 'writing a book'.)

OK, lecture over. You shouldn't even still be reading.

Aux armes, citoyens. Aux armes, citoyennes.

Harry

PS: I'm human; this is an email. Hit reply and knock yourself out. (Though, please, not literally.)

PPS: You want guidance? We got guidance. We're a blooming Guidance Factory. If you stuffed Jane Austen and Ernest Hemingway into a liquidiser, blitzed them up, then added Juice of Publisher, Zest of Indie-dom, and a few drops of blood from the Masked Lexicographer himself – you'd make something that was like us, *only not quite as good*.

The gateway to our magical kingdom lies on our website. We built the JW club to solve the kind of problems that writers have. And you're a writer.

PPPS: Hate these emails? Don't want to be a writer? Prefer to try ironing your head with a warm brick? Then unsubscribe.

Feeling doomy?

Writers have a tough gig in some ways. We're asked to be creative professionals, all daydreams and alternate worlds, but we also have to live in an industry which is changing fast, which delivers terrible and declining incomes, and where the writer is, in most industry situations, the least informed and least powerful person in the room.

Not easy, right?

There's one huge qualification to that, of course. Traditionally published authors *have* faced a severe decline in income and they *do* struggle for authority in their own industry. I don't like either of those things and neither agents nor authors associations have done enough to fight back.

But that's trad authors, and they're now in a minority.

For indies, making a meaningful income is absolutely possible. There are thousands of indies making a viable full-time living from the pen, more now than ever before in history. As for power – well, it's easy to be the most powerful person in the room, when you're the only person in it.

Even so, there are a couple of memes doing the rounds at the moment suggesting that the outlook is darkening for everyone: trad, indie, hybrid.

Argument one: pricing e-books at 99c/99p used to deliver a real kick to sales. That kick has almost completely vanished. The days of being able to promote successfully on Amazon have gone.

Argument two: Amazon's new emphasis on ads has created a 'pay to play' requirement for authors. In effect, if you want Amazon to sell your book, you have to pay it to do so, and that fat 70% royalty you get starts to drain back into Jeff Bezos's pocket.

So what do we think? What do *you* think?

On the first matter, it's certainly true that low pricing is now so common that simply dropping a price overnight achieves almost nothing.

But low pricing *alone* is, and always has been, an unbelievably dumb strategy. It's like a price promotion without the element of actual promotion.

If a clothes retailer wants to shift some winter dresses, they'll put the dresses in the front window with a big red banner yelling 'SALE'. Price cut plus promotion equals sales. It's obvious, isn't it?

Introduce the same price cut, but display the dresses in a back room on the top floor, and you won't shift the stock. Which is why no one – except trad publishers – takes that approach.

Any smart indie knows that promos work when you *promote*. That means using price cuts plus some combination of:

- Email marketing.
- Book discount sites.
- Facebook ads.
- Bookbub ads.
- Cross-promos with other authors.
- Whole series promos.
- Kindle Countdown deals.

You don't need to use all those every time, but you select from that basic menu to add jet fuel to your promo.

And it works. Of course it does. Always did, always will.

(Oh, and if you're wondering why Amazon advertising isn't on that list, it's because Amazon ads are weirdly unsuitable for big Amazon promotions. They work fine as evergreen drip-style marketing. They don't work for the big-surge type ads needed to grab visibility around a promo. If you're incredibly clever and talented, though, you may even have figured a way around that issue.)

In short, the death-by-overcrowding of the 99c ebook is merely the death of the Stupid Non-Promoting Promotion. And who cares about that? Not you. Not me.

The other issue – the 'pay to play' one – *is* more concerning.

Amazon is now pretty much forcing indies to advertise their books. (Big Publishers too, except that they're nervous of going all-in, so they do much less than they should.) And yes: that need to advertise is cutting indies' margins. That's bad.

But then again: Amazon ads have always been frustratingly useless. Profitable, yes, but hard to scale. The recent set of changes has made those ads much more viable than they used to be. And since trad publishers remain cautious about giving money to the beast, that just means that the playing field has shifted (again) in favour of indies.

In short, I'm not too concerned.

But even to talk about all this reminds us that, in today's world, the author can no longer afford to be passive. Finding an agent, finding a publisher, then closing your eyes – that strategy was never smart, but now it's pretty near suicidal.

The old rules are still the best rules:

Write well. Get informed ... and have fun.

Harry

PS: I'm human, this is an email. If you want to reply to me, you know what to do.

PPS: Hate these emails? Don't want to be a writer? Prefer to try ironing your head with a warm brick? Then unsubscribe.

The comfort again and again of writing something fictional down

A poet, Hannah Sullivan, just won the T.S. Eliot Prize for Poetry, for *Three Poems*. It included these lines:

> *Tears and liver spots on the back of the hand,*
> *The comfort again and again of writing something*
>   *fictional down.*

And that caught my eye. Last week's email was entitled 'Feeling doomy?' and comprised a whole lot of yadda about price promos and Amazon ads and stuff that has nothing whatsoever to do with writing and the pleasure of writing.

So this week: we're on pleasure patrol. We're just going to have a nice time.

That thing about killing darlings? Well, it's a load of old rubbish, no matter what. (Why kill your darlings? They're often the best bits in the book.) So today, we're just going to get our darlings out and give 'em a cuddle.

And here, in no especial order, are some bits from my Fiona books that I like and my reasons for liking them.

From *Talking to the Dead*

The narrator, my detective Fiona Griffiths, visits her mother. She says:

> *We eat ham, carrots and boiled potatoes, and watch a TV chef telling us how to bake sea bream in the Spanish fashion.*

I like that, simple as it is, because it tells you so much about Fiona's mother and her relationship and does so without saying anything directly.

So Fiona's mother cooks and eats ham, carrots and boiled potatoes, which is about as plain and traditional a meal as it's possible to get. But she watches a TV cookery show that tells her how to cook something she clearly isn't going to make. (If she was the kind of person to prepare sea bream Spanish-style, she wouldn't be eating ham, carrots and spuds.)

Now it might look like Fiona doesn't make any comment about this directly ... except she does.

She does it partly by the juxtaposition. But also that phrase, 'in the Spanish fashion'. That's a slightly pompous, over-mannered phrase, and Fiona is generally very unpompous. In effect, that use of language is Fiona's way of raising an eyebrow at the contrast. And all that without passing any comment directly.

So one plain and easy sentence tells us about the mother, about Fiona, and what they do and don't share with each other. Yum.

From *Love Story, with Murders*
Fiona's in a remote cottage on an exceptionally cold night. Here's how she reports it:

> *It's like the entire world is being tightened up. Waterfalls are being frozen into place, trees stiffened, the air clarified, the ground plated over with iron.*

That's writing that sounds more like writing. But I like it. The snippet takes that one idea (freezing = an act of tightening) and runs with it.

Waterfalls frozen into place: I like that. Waterfall normally calls to mind something in constant motion, and here it's being associated with the opposite. The ground plated over with iron: I like that too. It's common enough to say, 'the ground is like iron', but the 'plated over' bit calls attention to the transition from soft to hard.

And that transition has an edge, right? You can already feel the world getting slightly more dangerous. And do you want to guess whether Fiona has a calm and peaceful time in that cottage or whether something scary happens …?

Uh-oh.

From *The Strange Death of Fiona Griffiths*

Here, Fiona is undercover and she's just been 'arrested'. She needs to maintain her cover during the arrest process, so here (in part) is how she does it:

> *I have a brief interview with the duty solicitor. She seems like a nice woman – Barbara, mumsy, keen to help. I tell her to fuck off.*
>
> *Then sit without speaking for ten minutes.*
>
> *Then we're done.*

I like that too. You see the authentic Fiona, who assesses the duty solicitor in a warm, generous way (nice, mumsy, keen to help). And you see the undercover one, who just swears. The swearing is so abrupt, it's shocking. The sitting in silence is shocking too. And even, 'Then we're done.' There's a remarkable toughness in that whole way of behaving and that way of not talking about what's just happened.

The tiny little scene gains its vigour from our insight into the inner Fiona (who's relatable and generous) and the outer one, who's hard as nails. It's not just the solicitor who ends up a bit shocked. We do too.

And that whole scene took place in just thirty-six words. Even by Fiona's standards, that's abrupt.

From *This Thing of Darkness*

Here's a debrief scene, Fiona with her commanding officer, Dennis Jackson:

'We've got a load more data now.' Jackson pushes a thick file over the desk at me. *'But nothing concrete, not yet.'*

I take the file. Sit with it on my lap.

I'm still half in holiday mode, so I'm wearing stuff more summery, more playful than I'd usually wear to the office. A sleeveless dress in sky blue and sandals that show off my red toes.

Jackson nods at my hand. It's much better now, but I still have a dressing on it.

'You hurt your hand,' he says, *exhibiting the observational prowess of a seasoned officer.*

'Yes, sir. I splidged myself in a car door.'

'Did you now?'

'Sir? That stuff in Rhayader. You and DI Watkins. I want to say that I really appreciate the way you handled that. I couldn't have managed it if we'd gone down official routes. So thank you. You really helped.'

I like this just because of the scene's elasticity and movement. We start (1) with a file full of data and a police problem to be solved.

But Fiona ignores the data, and just sits there (2) reflecting on her holiday outfit.

(3) Jackson calls attention to her wounded hand and Fiona ducks away from the question with a made-up word ('splidged') and a made-up event. (Needless to say, she did not hurt her hand in a car door. She hurt it while causing a large fishing trawler to sink in the midst of an Atlantic gale.)

(4) Jackson tosses out a sceptical, 'Did you now?' but doesn't pursue his scepticism.

(5) Fiona just changes the subject and (for a page or two) Jackson appears to accept the change.

That's four or five beats in the space of a hundred and fifty words, but the scene doesn't seem jerky; it just seems quite intimate. Only two people who know each other well can operate quite like that.

And then there's the surface glitter that comes from Fiona just being Fiona. (Her use of the word 'splidged'. Her comment about the observational prowess of a seasoned officer. That little thank-you speech of hers at the end, which might sound just like a thank you, except that she is also trying to shift the conversation away from the awkward subject of her damaged hand.)

As ever with Fiona, nothing is ever very dependable.

That's probably enough of my darlings for one week. But some minor thoughts with which to finish:

Don't kill your darlings. Most of them are probably lovely.

Do look closely at your darlings. If you understand why they work well on the page, you will increase your self-editing muscle by 0.001%. Do that kind of thing enough times and you'll be the Schwarzenegger of the self-edits.

Enjoy your darlings. Writing is hard. We're not meant to take public pleasure from looking at our work and saying, 'You know what? That's OK, that is.' But who cares? Let's just take our pleasures where we can. And if something is good, then think it and say it. You'll feel happier and you'll want to write more.

The comfort again and again of writing something fictional down.

Then reading it back.

Yum.

Harry

PS: Hit reply. Tell me about your darlings. Oh – and I've just had an idea. Tell me about your darlings, and in next week's email, I'll just collect a few of them together and say why I liked them. Don't send me stuff if you don't want it made public though.

PPS: We're building a real proper community site for writers at the moment. When that's done, we might shift the post-email chat over there for follow-up. But for now, the reply button is your friend.

PPPS: Crochet is good, right? Writing is BAD. Writing makes you look like Jack Nicholson in *The Shining*. So unsubscribe right now this minute. Crochet is better.

A parcel of darlings

Last week, I got to cavort around reading you bits of my text. This week, the fur-lined slipper is on the other foot. You lot are behind the wheel and there's a wicked gleam in your eye.

Oh, and do watch out for the PSs over the next week or few: we've got some good things lined up and I want to tell you all about them. But for now, here are your darlings – a short selection:

From *Donny*, by Mick Wilson

I'm sat in the gulch, chewing a bone, when I see him, all raggedy. He shows me the thing he's got. It's brass, a little chunky figure.

'This is Donny,' he says. 'Like Buddha, but stupid hair. You wanna buy?' I run the Geiger across it. It's clean.

'Why?' I say.

My comment:
This is just excellent. I like the word *gulch*, an unusual and arresting word right off the bat.

I like the '*chewing a bone*', and especially the way that isn't questioned or explained.

And I like '*see him, all raggedy.*' What I particularly like there is the way the grammar loosens up around the word *raggedy*. A more formal construction would be something like, 'I see him, a ragged man in his late thirties.' Or: 'I see him. He is ragged and [sun-burned or old or whatever else].' By contrast, '*all raggedy*' feels hastily, almost clumsily put together. It's a raggedy sentence-ending, which – given what's being described – is pitch perfect.

And then the dialogue is all solid gold too. We jump from *Donny* (which has one kind of feel for us), to *Buddha*, which feels abruptly different, then to *stupid hair*, which re-orients us again. That's two sudden jumps in eight words, and the effect is to keep the reader paying very close attention to each word, because we have no idea where we're going next.

The little surprises keep popping too. We might semi-expect the '*You wanna buy*', but then we definitely weren't expecting the Geiger counter. And, after the item has shown up as clean of radioactivity, we might expect the purchase negotiation to continue, but no. We get the question '*why?*', which isn't the one we wanted to ask, but now that it has been asked, we very much want to know what the answer is.

Verdict:

If I were an agent and this were a novel (which it isn't; it's from a short story), I'd be very interested indeed. This is outstanding.

From *Untitled*, by David Congreave

(Well, OK, it probably isn't untitled. I just don't know what the title is.) But here's the chunk:

> *'Kitten, go back inside, there's a giant crow out here.'*
>
> *Kitten visibly perked up. She'd never met a bird that was too big to chase and, while a crow was nearing the limits of her avian-killing capabilities, she felt up to the challenge. A breakfast of tinned stewing steak and a pleasant nap had given Kitten the bravado to attempt to slaughter an entire murder of crows.*
>
> *She bounded the rest of the way through the cat flap and sniffed the air eagerly, hoping to catch the scent of oily feathers. But it quickly became clear that there were no birds, or indeed anything warm and chase-able, in the vicinity. Kitten looked at Pip with the same expression that a child might use after being promised chocolate cake and instead handed a bowl of sprouts.*

My comment:

This is also strong.

I like the set-up: Pip teasing Kitten. I like some of the phrase-making: a *murder of crows*, and (especially) those *oily* feathers. The punchline is strong too. It's not just that Kitten feels disappointed here; there's a hint that a betrayal of trust has taken place. Kitten trusted Pip and Pip let her down. This isn't just a punchline, there's an emotional transition.

All that is strong. For me, though, some of the language feels a little overcooked. (Bear in mind, that I'm very, very picky about these things. I'm worse than at least 90% of the agents out there.) So which of these feels more fluid? More readable?

- (A) She'd never met a bird that was too big to chase and, while a crow was nearing the limits of her avian-killing capabilities, she felt up to the challenge.
- (B) She'd never met a bird that was too big to chase and, while a crow (a giant one, no less) would hardly make for an easy kill, she felt up to the challenge.

To my ear, the 'avian-killing capabilities' phrase seems a little too adult, a little too heavy-handed for the story actually being told. I'd probably shorten the next sentence too, and for similar reasons. Those are editing tweaks, though. One quick pass would fix everything.

Verdict:

I'd want the language to attune to the story a little more, but the needle's already hovering at 'serious potential'. (Though on a pure marketing point, agents tend to avoid stories about talking animals, except for the very youngest readers. I've no idea what kind of book this actually is, though.)

From *The Go-Giver Influencer*, by John Mann and Bob Burg

Interesting one, this, as John told me a little about how he got to the line I'm about to quote. Here's what he says:

'Chapter two picks the story up from [Gillian's] point of view – and I wanted to thrust the reader into her perspective, to experience a bit of a jolt from seeing her as a hostile force [which is how she appears in chapter 1] to suddenly understanding how the world looks through her eyes. Which is that she desperately needs to secure Jackson's account to gain a promotion she wants … In a sense, overly simplified, the message of the book is 'put yourself in the other person's shoes'. Rather than preach that, I wanted to have the reader experience it, by pulling them up out of Jackson's perspective and sitting them down in Ms. Waters's. So I wanted to open with a first line that put us directly inside Gillian's struggle, yet also perfectly echoed and mirrored Jackson's.'

And here's that chapter 2 opening sentence:

> *Gillian stared out her office window, trying to see her future.*

My comment:
Bam! Perfect. The first six words there are tedious. The next four words aren't promising. That final word detonates the whole sentence into life.

We know that she can't see a future, certainly not in this literal, out-of-an-office-window way. But we also know exactly what John means: that way we use this kind of day-dreaming to pick away at little life problems. The contradiction opens and immediately resolves.

The sentence does more than that, though. Gillian is presented as an office worker, but there's already a sense of her straining to escape. Wanting more. Indeed, we've got the entire story set-up already laid out for us. So in an unflashy and highly economical way, John delivers all that. In eleven words.

Verdict:
John said in his email to me that this wasn't 'Pulitzer Prize prose.' Well, isn't it? I mean, you have to write more than eleven words to win a Pulitzer, but there's nothing at all wrong with those eleven. I would say that if I were an agent, I'd be pretty damn interested in this writing ... except, if I were, I'd be too late. John mentioned that the book was already out, so I checked it out. It's out with Penguin and is co-authored with a NYT bestseller. Quality shows.

From *Love Not Included*, by Hazel Allbut

Robert rose from the sofa as she entered the room. His defensive manner had disappeared, and his voice had softened.

Ava had never felt so terrified.

<u>My comment:</u>

This is simple-bimple, right? Nothing fancy, nothing tricksy.

But it also goes to show that emotional deftness, conveyed in clear language, can deliver plenty for the reader. And the whole passage relies on that little ambush in the final word. This guy is standing up, undefended, soft-voiced. We're expecting something comforting, right? But no. There's something terrifying here and the reader instantly wants to know what and why.

I would say that even this tiny passage could use a wash-and-brush-up type edit. The passage would work just as well like this:

Robert rose as she entered. His defensive manner had disappeared and his voice was soft. [note that I've deleted that unnecessary comma.]
Ava had never felt so terrified.

That's the same thing, but I've deleted the needless '*from the sofa*' and '*the room*', and I've replaced '*softened*' with '*soft*'. A thirty-word sentence has become a twenty-five-word one, and the actual felt-saving is a bit better than that, because the comma and the '*softened*' were adding micro-delays of their own.

Now, OK, I know what you're thinking: 'Harry, really, that's five words. Five. Just what kind of a pedant are you?'

Well, I'm a really pedantic one. Like really, really pedantic. Five words added to a twenty-five-word sentence is the equivalent of 20,000 words added to a 100,000-word novel. A novel that baggy shouldn't be published and probably wouldn't be. And you have to look for economy at every single level of your prose: sentence, paragraph, scene, chapter. Only by rooting out anything unnecessary do you reach the right level of tightness.

OK, sermon over.

Verdict:

Great stuff. Tighten up the writing, but I already want to know what happens next.

That's it from me. Check out the PSs. See you next week.

Harry, the Pedant of Pedant Hall

PS: Hit reply. Talk to me.

PPS: You like videos, right? You like writing, yes? So videos about writing and publishing – that's like your own private heaven. Feast your eyes and treat your ears to these little beauties on our YouTube channel:

Self-publishing your e-book [a good simple overview].

10 great writing tips from great writers (+ 10 terrible ones).

7 different ways to plot a novel.

We've got some other cracking films in the pipeline. More on that soon.

PPPS: Only just realised that I'm a terrible pedant? Terrified you might turn out the same way? Unsubscribe to this email thread and escape now.

A faster horse

So: big response to the parcel of darlings email last week. I've still got a lot of people to reply to, so please just bear with me if you wrote to me and haven't yet heard back.

And yes: we'll do that again sometime soon. Partly it's just nice sharing our darlings, but also a lot of you found my editorial-type comments helpful. And there's no question that close attention to details of actual sentence construction is THE single most important self-editing skill there is. Every single aspect of a book improves as a result, even the big machinery of plot and character.

So yes: I'll just make that feedback-and-celebration slot a regular feature of this email.

As for today?

Well, I've got a cold. The kids are off school. (Snow!) And I don't especially feel in the zone for another 1500-word epic on some micro-aspect of writing or publishing.

So here's one small thought – but a useful one, I hope.

I've just seen a bunch of crime writers chatting online about whether to write third person or first person, and whether to write close third, or omniscient third, and what tense is OK, and so on. The writer who started the thread has already published (very successfully) in first person and was worried that readers might be upset at her changing mode.

And, look, I do think that the decisions you make on these things matters. My Fiona Griffiths novels simply wouldn't have been possible in third person. Or they'd have been possible, but a bit pointless. There's a way in which those books are all about Fiona's voice. That quality of being inside her head, completely and always.

Tense too. I don't like present tense as a rule, but writing in the present tense suits Fiona's voice, so bingo: I chose that tense. The books are better as a result.

But worrying about what readers might think? Or editors? Or agents?

No.

The only question you have to ask yourself is what your books want. What your characters need from you on this particular story.

Steve Jobs once said this:

Some people say, 'Give the customers what they want.' But that's not my approach. Our job is to figure out what they're going to want before they do. I think Henry Ford once said, 'If I'd asked customers what they wanted, they would have told me, "A faster horse!"' People don't know what they want until you show it to them. That's why I never rely on market research. Our task is to read things that are not yet on the page.

He's right.

Write a book that is startlingly good, and no reader will ever worry about first/third, present/past, multi-POV/single-POV, or close/omniscient.

I get why writers worry about those things. It's our job to get them right, and if we write a whole damn novel, then realise we've written it third person when we should have written it in first person – well, that's just a hell of a big mistake to correct.

But don't worry about others. Worry about your book. If the book wants a particular presentation, then go for it. I used to write third person/multi-POV/past tense, and readers loved that stuff. I now write first person/single-POV/present tense, and readers love that stuff too.

Market research? Bleah. Just write a great book.

Harry

PS: Hit reply. Talk to me.

PPS: Hate writing? Want to go and play in the snow? Go play. Escape this writing nonsense by unsubscribing to this thread here.

The taste of ash

I want to talk dust and ashes in this email – the nice, yummy, novelistic version of ash, that is.

You'll be familiar, of course, with the basic notion of structuring a novel.

You need some kind of status quo to open the book with. That may be basically positive (as in *Pride and Prejudice*, for example) or seriously negative (as in Emma Donoghue's *Room*, for example), but it's settled. It's not in motion.

Then along comes an Initiating Incident. The status quo is broken. The protagonist strives to accomplish some goal. He or she may win some battles, but they probably also lose some. Then, towards the end of the book, everything mounts up into some kind of crisis. Everything comes to be at stake. Then everything is resolved, for good or ill, tra-la.

Now that's all fine. Nothing new there. But what I want to tease open a bit more is that moment of crisis itself. In *Pride and Prejudice*, the crisis is precipitated by Lydia's disastrous elopement with the rascally Wickham. Her behaviour means the family will be dishonoured, so that none of the girls will be able to make a decent marriage, which in turn means that they will all, before too long, be plunged into poverty. The bitterness of that catastrophe is particularly sharp, because Jane is now all set to be happily betrothed to the friendly-and-rich Mr Bingley, and Lizzie now has the hots for the all-round-good-guy (and spectacularly wealthy) Mr Darcy.

And because we novelists have to engineer our plot twists just so, we all have a tendency to focus hard on the externals of that crisis: What event could best ruin Lizzie's family? Where is she when she hears? How does Darcy get to hear? How is the thing resolved? Etc, etc.

But the externals are just like some mechanical parts that need proper bolting into place. Yes, you have to line up the bolts correctly, but the actual mechanics aren't overly interesting.

Where it gets more fun is with the character's internal dynamic.

Now it's pretty obvious that the character has to have a real 'Oh hell!' moment. The moment where everything seems reduced to dust and ash. Where all hope dies.

(And yes, that's obvious, but it is nevertheless always worth checking that you do properly register your protagonist's feelings. Don't just rely on the *externals* being bad. You also need the novelistic equivalent of the reaction shot – the point at which the character realises just how shite everything now is. In a more introspective, talky sort of book, that reaction shot may extend over pages. If your writing is more at the Lee Child end of the spectrum, the reaction shot – like the character – is likely to be a little more laconic. Either way is fine; just make sure you do it.)

But I wanted to raise something else too.

In any really interesting book, the nature of the crisis, the nature of the character's own history, the nature of the character's goal and the nature of the character's own spiritual/emotional life challenge all form a beautiful and messy knot. They're not four separate elements; they're different manifestations of the book's underlying theme.

So in *Pride and Prejudice*, we have:

Nature of the crisis:
Lydia is immature. She makes a terrible romantic choice. She chooses the man who most embodies the opposite to Darcy's severe but upright morality.

Nature of Lizzie Bennet's own history:
She's immature. She made a terrible romantic choice (without ever following through. That's what keeps Lizzie and the book itself in play.) She came close to choosing the man who most embodies the opposite to Darcy's severe but upright morality. Faced with a direct marriage proposal from severe-and-upright Darcy, she said no.

Nature of Lizzie Bennet's goal:
To make the right romantic choice. To marry a good man. (And, OK, it would be kind of nice if he was a billionaire as well.)

Nature of Lizzie Bennet's spiritual/emotional life challenge:
To grow up. To stop being immature. To make sober, unprejudiced judgements of other humans.

Put like that, you can instantly see that the whole 'dust and ashes' moment in the book – the moment of ultimate crisis – is a device that brings ALL the themes of the book into focus at the one same time. If the 'dust and ashes' moment is nothing more than 'Oh shit, I've wandered into a trap and now the bad guy is going to kill me,' it's more or less certain that the book will be instantly forgettable. And yes, it's possible to make a living from efficiently engineered, but basically soulless, writing. But (A) you'll sell more books and make more money by adding some depth to all that efficient engineering. And (B) who wants to spend their time writing basically forgettable books? Not you. Not me. That's not why we do what we do.

Oh, and although that moment of crisis brings these things into pinprick-sharp focus, in any really good book, you'll find the same themes infiltrating things pretty much everywhere. So for example:

Nature of Lizzie's father's journey:
Lizzie's father is literate and witty and ironic. But his tragic flaw is a kind of emotional pas-

sivity. He merely observes at times when he ought to act. He is, in fact, immature, and that immaturity is what gave rise to Lydia's disastrous elopement. Darcy's combination of intelligent observation and willingness to take action looks even better by contrast.

Nature of the Charlotte/Mr Collins subplot:

Charlotte is emotionally mature. She makes a sensible choice (to marry the ridiculous, but prosperous, Mr Collins.) But she marries without love, and that represents a choice that the more passionate Lizzie cannot make.

In short, understanding the 'dust and ashes' moment becomes a way to understand the deeper channels of your book itself. And when you get that understanding, you may find yourself wanting to tweak things to make the various web of connections that little bit denser and more interesting.

And as for the dust and ashes moment itself – well, I have to say, writing that stuff has long given me some of my very yummiest writing experiences. Call me sadistic if you like, but I relish that ability to plunge my character into the deepest turmoil I can contrive. Enough of Mr Nice Guy. Let's all go be mean to our protagonists.

★★ Evil cackle ★★

Harry

PS: I'm a human. Hit reply and see what happens.

PPS: YouTube used to be all funny cats and inexplicably popular teenage vloggers. And now, it's cats, vloggers, and me talking about defining your genre. In other words: YouTube just got better.

PPPS: Hate writing? Prefer to learn dry stone walling or the fine art of falconry? Then unsubscribe to this email thread now.

Giants and gentlefolk

The theory of these emails is simple. It is:

(A) Include useful actionable content in the body of the email.
(B) Ensure that the content relates to writing, publishing, and all that.
(C) Stuff some promotional type stuff in the PSs, so it's there for anyone who wants it.

The key word in all that is 'actionable' – and this email is going to break that promise. Or at least, it probably is.

Because what I want to talk about is the birth of the novel. Leaving aside works in other languages, the leading contenders for title of First Novel in the English Language are probably John Bunyan's *The Pilgrim's Progress* (1678), Aphra Behn's *Oroonoko* (1688), and Daniel Defoe's *Robinson Crusoe* (1722).

Personally, Bunyan's book doesn't ring my novelistic bell, which means it's a straightforward punch-up between Behn and Defoe – who were both (weird fact) secret agents as well as writers. Either way, the novel itself wasn't born until 1700, give or take, or a good century after Shakespeare was in his prime, three hundred years after Chaucer, and possibly as many as a thousand years after *Beowulf*.

And that's a pretty startling thought, isn't it?

Whoever wrote *Beowulf* was pretty dedicated to telling a story. Yes, that story had some slightly weird (to us) digressions, but still most of what we expect to see in a novel was already there. A hero. An antagonist. A beginning, middle and end. A biff-bam climax with a satisfying amount of gore.

You have to wonder what took so long for *Beowulf*-type writing to progress to *Robinson Crusoe*-type writing? Why not do the obvious thing and jump straight to long prose stories which are, apart from anything else, a damn sight easier to write?

Well, there are a bunch of theories here, and they're not mutually exclusive. For one thing, poems like *Beowulf* were composed as entertainment for kings. That was how they found their market. That's how the writer got paid.

Novels were never like that. They were printed up and sold in very much the same way that novels today are sold. So for the economics to work out, the price of paper and printing had to come right down; the number of literate people with cash to spare had to jump right up. Early eighteenth-century Britain hadn't yet started to industrialise, but it was already the wealthiest corner of the globe and had allowed its censorship laws to collapse. If the novel was going to take off anywhere, the bustle of modern London looked like a pretty good bet.

But that's only to look at externals. Something internal was happening too.

Beowulf, remember, is a story of a hero fighting a monster. The work of Shakespeare is stuffed full of ghosts (*Hamlet* and *Macbeth*), witches (*Macbeth*), and indeed wizards, monsters and some really terrible fairies (*The Tempest*). Those mythical story elements stretch right back to the *Iliad* and before.

Nor is it just the mythical creatures. The protagonists of most of this pre-novel storytelling were more like archetypes than true individuals. I don't count Bunyan's *Pilgrim's Progress* as a novel, precisely because his characters were two-dimensional cardboard cutouts. That was their whole *purpose*, in fact: to represent types, not delineate individuals.

Yet by the time you get to *Robinson Crusoe*, those archetypes have vanished completely. *Robinson Crusoe* is no longer a type. He's a person. As you read the novel, you feel like you know him. You could have a perfectly sensible argument about which Hollywood actor should best play him.

The individual had taken his or her place at the heart of story. The novel was born. You, dear reader, follow in that 300-year tradition.

Now that's all well and good. If you ask me, it's also bloody interesting and thought-provoking. (For example: does it feel different to be human now than it did a thousand years ago? Do we get our own sense of individuality, in part, from having had so many storytellers explain to us what it is to be individual? I don't know, but I'd guess yes.)

Now, OK, these emails are supposed to be at least a little bit actionable, and I haven't yet given you anything you can scrape your claws on. But let me see if I can offer you something, all the same.

When authors of science fiction or fantasy (SFF) start to send their work out to literary agents, they'll encounter a weird number of agents who basically accept any kind of genre under the sun, except SFF.

And I always think, *huh?* So a very short list of work that those agents presumably hate would include:

- Margaret Atwood's *The Handmaid's Tale*.
- Aldous Huxley's *Brave New World*.
- Kurt Vonnegut's *Slaughterhouse Five*.
- George Orwell's *1984*.
- All of *Harry Potter*.
- *Macbeth, Hamlet, The Tempest*, and plenty of other Shakespeare plays.
- The *Iliad*, the *Odyssey, Beowulf, Le Morte D'Arthur*, and about a bazillion other classic, classic texts.

So those agents must be stupid, or maybe they just hate English literature. Except they're probably not stupid and most of them have English degrees. So what's going on?

Here's what I think the deal is – and what it means for you.

Most agents love the Robinson Crusoe-ish tradition. They want their novels to be true novels, shorn of myth and archetypes. That's why they come over all weird when they get a touch of the Gandalfs. They don't *want* wise men with staffs. They don't *want* the archetypes. That's not why they become agents.

Other agents are more catholic in their tastes. (And, I think, better readers as a result.) Yes, they like the novelistic tradition, but they also enjoy it when a modern novelist hurtles into the older, mythical tradition and causes a great genre-mixing rumpus.

So, for example, when Neil Gaiman writes *American Gods*, he's borrowing the strength and majesty and power of those old archetypes ... but he's also ramming those archetypes with a genuinely modern, individual hero, and plenty of wicked, very modern mischief-making. It's a brilliant combination.

Implications for you? I think they're twofold.

Let's say you do have some fantastical elements in your work (a dystopia, a near-future world, a ghost, some time-travel, anything like that). Well, if you don't want your novel to be shelved with SFF and viewed as a pure fantasy work, then:

- You need to make damn sure that your protagonist is a carefully drawn individual.
- You probably need to make sure that all the other characters are as well.
- You need to write reasonably well.

Do those things and you can happily send your work to agents, even if those agents say 'no SFF'. They won't even get worried about the fantasy elements you do have, because they'll understand that you're a member of Team Crusoe not Team Beowulf.

If, on the other hand, you do want to follow the Neil Gaiman route – that is, if your novel is a proper fusion of the mythic tradition and the modern tradition – then you need to go for it. Specifically:

- You need to bring some proper, big mythic elements into your work.
- Your protagonist, however, needs to be a carefully drawn individual (even if he/she feels like an everyman/everywoman).
- You need to know your genre. If you are writing true SFF, you can't not know what other people are writing in this field. You can't be ignorant of its history.
- You need to have fun – no point in playing this game otherwise.

Do that, and not only will there be at least some agents who love your work, but you'll find plenty of hyper-engaged and enthusiastic readers too. Oh yes, and your storytelling tradition is at least 4,000 years old, or 3,700 years older than the Team Crusoe one, so you live in good company.

That's all from me.

Till next week.

Harry

PS: I'm a human. Hit reply and see what happens.

PPS: Hate writing? So do I. Then unsubscribe to this email thread now and let's sulk together.

Hiccupy starts and some simple rules

A few Festivals back, our keynote author was the extremely wonderful Antonia Hodgson. Her first book (a historical murder story) was an award-winner and a bestseller and launched Antonia's very successful subsequent career.

So I introduced her, much as you'd expect. Roughly: 'Here's the lavishly successful Antonia. We can all drip with envy at what she's achieved.'

Then she started her talk. What she said was good, interesting, useful stuff, but I could sense that the audience wasn't completely engaged. And I thought I knew what the problem was as well. Because Antonia wasn't just a novelist; she was editor-in-chief at Little, Brown.

To our delegates, I think it felt a little bit like of course you could have a smash-hit bestseller ... as long as you had the good sense to make sure you were the chief editor at a major publisher first. It's like our audience was dutifully recording Antonia's wise advice but didn't actually feel connected with her or her experience.

Then, ten minutes in, it all changed. Antonia turned to me and said, 'Oh, and by the way, Harry,

The Devil in the Marshalsea wasn't my first novel. It was my first *published* novel.'

Instantly, the energy in that room altered. All of a sudden, you could feel the audience thinking, 'Oh! That's like me!' And sure enough, Antonia told a brilliant – and true – story about the novel that had preceded *The Devil* – a 250,000-word monster novel about vampires that was too long, too baggy, and had missed the whole vampire wave by about a million years.

Basically, Antonia's first novel was a balls-up. And yes, because of who she was, she had an agent for that balls-up, but that agent didn't even try to sell the book. He just told her it was unsaleable and she should go away and write one that wasn't.

Good advice, right? (And imagine saying that to the editor-in-chief of Little, Brown …)

Anyway. That was Antonia's story.

My story is the same but different.

So: my first ever book found an agent without too much fuss. It found a publisher via a highly contested auction. And it became a bestseller. And it sold in loads of places round the world.

Boom! I was a writer. And I had to be quite a good one, right, because of all that bestsellerishness?

So then I wrote my second book, utterly confident in my own brilliance. And the manuscript was terrible. Unpublishably bad.

My editor, very sweetly, told me this, and mostly managed to avoid swearing or breaking crockery or pulling too many of my fingernails out as he did so.

So I deleted the draft I'd delivered and rewrote that book from scratch. The new book did fine – prize-shortlisted, a film option, some big promotions – though I still can't quite think of it without remembering its terrible birth.

Anyway:

Two authors. Two successes. Two car crashes. Two hiccupy starts to otherwise successful careers.

And some lessons. If you want to distil them down, they're as follows:

1. Don't work with a shite idea

If your idea is terrible, it won't work, no matter what. Antonia's first book couldn't have worked. It wasn't a question of rewrites or new edits. It was a question of scrap it, move on.

My second book was a bit the same. The fundamental idea wasn't awful, perhaps, but it's like I had turned left out of the front door when I needed to turn right. There simply wasn't an editorial job to be done on my first draft, there was a delete-and-start-again job.

2. Build your technique

If your basic concept is strong enough, then *everything* comes down to your technique.

I don't mind if you think of that as your writing technique, or your self-editing technique. In the end, those things are the same. Some people hurl down a terrible first draft, then edit into shape. Others (like me) take care with the draft as they go, but that's only because my editing brain works right alongside my writing brain. I'll put a sentence down on the page, then rewrite it five times before moving on. And probably look at it another twenty or thirty or forty times before the book is actually done.

And look: technique is a matter of *knowing* stuff. How do plots work? How do characters work? Why do some scenes feel atmospheric and others feel bland? Why does a sentence sound strong one way and weak another way, even if it says essentially the same thing?

Those questions have answers – precise, rigorous, repeatable answers. And if you have managed to internalise that basic scaffolding of technique, then you'll hit many fewer problems as you write – and you'll solve them much faster too. I think you also enjoy writing more, because there's more flow and less frustration.

3. Keep at it

The oldest advice in the book, maybe, but it's vital all the same. If Antonia Hodgson had given up writing following her vampire disappointment, she wouldn't have the golden career she has today. If I'd walked off in a huff after my book #2 car crash, I wouldn't have had the life I've had for the last fifteen and more years.

Sometimes you get success with your first novel. Sometimes it just takes longer than that. But (duh!) you can't win unless you're still at the table.

And that's it really. Novel-writing in a nutshell. Till soon.

Harry

PS: I'm a human. Hit reply and see what happens.

PPS: Hate writing? Let's build an underground lair and hatch a Wicked Plan. Unsubscribe to this email thread first, though.

Home baking and that all-important church fete

Ha! Every now and then I get an email from a writer that opens up my Little Box of Annoyances. I don't mean that the writer themself is annoying; just that they remind me I've got something good to be annoyed about. And today's subject is a good 'un.

So. The writer's email said:

I did a creative writing course [run by a first-class literary agency] eighteen months ago, and I have had some feedback from a couple of agents that they have liked my writing. (In your terms, I think I've been doing reasonably ok with the 'execution'.) Where I think I've been having difficulty is with the idea. I wrote a political thriller last year with lots of deliberately unappealing characters all stabbing each other in the back – but the trouble with that was feedback that I had too many unappealing characters, the market being more comfortable with appealing characters.

So the writer thinks, OK, I can write, but I need to write something more mainstream/appealing, so he does so, and gets (thus far at least) little positive response to that one either.

Brilliant.

Now, there are a couple of things I want to address there, but the one I want to pick on today is that whole issue of 'too many unappealing characters'. It's as though agents are looking through a book and saying, 'Hmm, this is a great book, but there's no one involved in home baking. Nobody is volunteering for the church fete. And – hey, we're Literary Professionals, so we know these things – readers won't read a book if characters don't do their bit for the church fete, so, regretfully, we'll have to pass.'

This theory – let's call it the Home Baking Hypothesis – is horseshit, of course. (Pardon the language, but I have opened my Little Box of Annoyances, so these things happen.)

To prove the failure of the HBH, pick up a copy of *American Psycho*. That's right: I'm talking about the massively bestselling, modern classic, movie-adapted book by Brett Easton Ellis. Now the central character there – the first-person narrator, no less – is not just vain, not just a psychopath, not just a multiple murderer, but WORSE STILL he is an investment banker. He does not put on his pinny and bake cupcakes for the church fete. He kills people, gorily.

So agents should hate his book, right? No home baking, ergo no readers.

Except – duh – see above in relation to (a) bestsellerdom, (b) modern classicdom, and (c) movie adaptation.

So the whole appealing-character thing either has an investment-banker-shaped exemption in it (not probable), or the entire theory is rubbish.

Well: you already know what I think. And I have to say, my own experience bears this out.

I don't write any character as horrible as Easton Ellis's Bateman, but my most successful character – Fiona Griffiths – is successful *partly because I ensure she continues to annoy and disconcert my readers*.

So she smokes weed, illegally; she has a very dubious relationship with corpses (not sexual, but still alarming); she routinely annoys or mildly injures people who don't deserve it in any way at all; and much else.

In short, while there's a lot to like and admire in Fiona, she'll constantly needle you out of any complacently admiring state. She's admirable AND annoying AND disconcerting. All those three things, always.

Now, it's true that when my agent and I were looking to sell that series, we had plenty of rejections from publishers because they were alarmed at the whole no-home-baking vibe. But it's also true that we sold the book to every major market in the world, and usually to the leading crime publishers in those territories. The series has also been bought for TV – not once, but twice. That outcome wasn't despite the whole annoying/disconcerting thing, but because of it.

In short, the Home Baking Hypothesis is a stupid one. It's wrong. It's not true. You can forget it.

Except …

Except that agents aren't normally *completely* wrong. There's generally a fair-sized seed of truth in their concerns.

So.

Readers want story, but to engage with story, they have to be highly engaged with the main character. In a transition that only long-form fiction truly achieves, the reader has to (kind of) *become* the protagonist.

There are roughly two sorts of character you can ask your reader to become. They are:

Everyman/everywoman type characters. Erotica authors talk about 'self-insert' characters, meaning blank spaces on which the reader can carve their own initials. The term is ugly, but informative – and it turns out that characters of this sort are extremely common in fiction. Even Harry Potter, a wizard, is really an everyman character – just look at the start of the HP series, which depicts an ordinary boy bewildered by events.

The one-in-a-million bunch. That's Easton Ellis's Bateman. It's my Fiona Griffiths. It's Bridget Jones. It's Larsson's Lisbeth Salander. It's anyone who could cause an upheaval in an empty room.

Let's deal with that second type of character first. Yes, your reader somehow merges with your character, but they maintain a kind of dual perspective.

Partly, they inhabit (say) Lisbeth Salander with a kind of wild excitement. '*I'd* never do this in real life, but this *isn't* real life, so let's just have some fun …' Yet the reader's own perspective never completely vanishes. So when Salander then does something particularly shocking, the reader kind of peeps through their fingers at whatever's going on. 'I'd never do this, and this character should definitely not be doing this, but I can't help wanting to know where this is all going to end, so …'

It's the discordance between those two perspectives that gives these characters their kick. It's why I never let my Fiona settle into someone the reader can simply like.

The secret of writing great characters of this kind? Simply this: *entice* your reader into sharing your character's viewpoint, however awful, then buckle up and enjoy the ride. The reason why *American Psycho* works is because we completely inhabit Bateman. We know he's awful, but we can't bear to look away. (Strong writing is pretty crucial here. And, for obvious reasons, you'll find a lot of those characters come via first-person narration.)

With the everyman/everywoman character, you can have them be pretty good, or not very good, or just an ordinary bunch of flaws and virtues. Any approach you take is fine. But *you have to allow room for that self-insert process to take place.* You have to enable your reader to make the leap.

That means:

Good writing, of course.

You can't, as author/narrator, drip with contempt for your own characters. You have to sort of like them, however unlikeable they are. If you treat your characters with contempt, your reader will sense it and that merging of character and reader will not take place.

You make sure that your character wrestles with flaws and challenges. They can be morally dubious, or even bad, but the reader has to see some kind of inner conflict – something the character worries about or wants to do better at.

Here's a simple example by way of illustration.

My first book, *The Money Makers*, dealt with three seriously flawed brothers, each of whom accounted for roughly one third of the total page space in the book. One of these guys was just a baddy – ambitious, manipulative, clever, bad. The second was morally weak – kept making the wrong choices – but he felt bad about letting down one girlfriend, was really anxious to make things work with another, and genuinely sought to master his profession, with the aim of excelling. The third guy was also weak, but started the reform process about midway through the book, and ended up a proper, courageous, through-and-through good guy.

If I'd populated the book only with out-and-out baddies, it wouldn't have worked. It was the presence of two flawed-but-trying humans (at different stages of their progression towards the light) that gave ordinary readers their entrance into the book. Oh, and even the out-and-out baddy had a kind of repentance and renewal right at the end. It took time, but he too *felt* the conflict.

Technically, that book was about three unappealing characters, all willing to lie, cheat and betray. But it sold to publishers in a massively contested auction and became a bestseller.

The Home Baking Hypothesis? Forget about it. Getting your reader to merge with your characters? Absolutely vital.

Next week: I re-open my Little Box of Annoyances, and we'll see what springs out.

Till then.

Harry

PS: Got something to tell me? Well, heck: I am a human and this is an email …

PPS: 'When will we get word of the Festival of Writing?' you ask, in a manner convenient for an author composing some promotional email PSs.

'Soon!' comes my convenient-yet-evasive reply. 'It's going to be great.'

(That's marketing gold, that is.)

PPPS: Hate writing? Want to go and solve the Riddle of Brexit? You'd better unsubscribe to this email thread and do what needs to be done.

Do you write from the heart, Harry?

The subject of this week's missive comes from an email sent to me by a writer – let's call him Alessandro. The complete text of his email was simply this:

Do you write from the heart, Harry?

My answer was: *Yes, I do. I think everyone should.*

But last week's email centred on the challenges faced by another writer – let's call him Zachary. He wrote one book that contained unappealing characters, and the book was rejected for that reason. So then he wrote another which was a mainstream police procedural and (at least so far) he's had troubles placing that because it's too safe. In his words:

So I wrote another book (a police procedural) with a more mainstream feel. I currently have the book out on submission but the feedback I have had so far (where I've been lucky enough to get any) is that the market is very crowded and I need more to make the book stand out. Seems to me that I have to try and write something which is both unique and pleasingly familiar. I don't think I've found the formula yet but when I look at other books actually on sale, I'm not sure I can always identify what's unique about them either.

If you're aiming at traditional publication, many of you will have had something like this experience. (Or, if your work isn't yet out on submission, that pleasure likely lies ahead.)

If you're self-publishing, then of course you can publish whatever you damn well please … but you still have that hard limit of what readers actually want. Books about unlovable politicians? Mainstream police procedurals without a stand-out hook? In a way, the very freedom of self-pub is also one of its bigger dangers: you could pump out three books in a series before you realised the data proved that series readthrough rates were unsustainably low. That would be a real yikes moment in any career.

So what do you do?

Write from your heart? Or write for the market? And if the latter, then how the heck do you know where the market actually is?

OK, well, to clarify my earlier statement that I think you 100% have to write from the heart, let me also add this: you absolutely have to write for the market. It's insane not to.

Imagine it as a big Venn diagram. The left-hand circle is All The Stories You'd Love To Write. The right-hand circle is All The Stories That Could Shift Some Books. The stuff you should write is plumb in the middle of that intersection. Whatever your genre, whatever your approach to market, that's where you should write.

Now, there are two common problems that writers face here.

Newer writers, especially those still engaged on their first ever novel, think, 'What do you mean, *all the stories I'd love to write*? I love THIS project. This is my heart's one true desire.'

But you know what? That's only because you're new to the game. If you love telling stories, then you'll find you can be equally gripped by a hundred other possible tales. It's a question of relaxing your attachment to whatever your current project is and letting yourself play with the other ideas as they come to you. The more you play with and explore those ideas, the richer and more exciting they'll seem.

So: simple problem, simple solution.

The other one is harder. The 'what do agents/editors/readers want?' question. And, to be clear, even agents – who are professional readers of and sellers to the market – can get this wrong. An agent can take on a project, genuinely loving its chances. Then they get it out on submission and find that editors don't agree. (Something I really loathe when it happens to our clients.)

So, accepting that this is a tough question, here are some rules of thumb:

Respect the rules
If you want to write a police procedural, then you need to do at least some of the basics in terms of

getting police ranks correct, procedural elements not wildly off, and so on. You can be pretty lax, in all honesty – I write police procedurals and my appetite for procedural research is fairly limited, to put it mildly. But you can't just trash the rules, not in any genre.

Same but different

You do offer *something* that stands out. Your book can't be just another entry in a genre. It has to zing in some way. In my case, with Fiona Griffiths, the zing is simply: 'Fiona is in recovery from Cotard's Syndrome, a real-life condition in which the sufferer believes themselves to be dead.' Boom! When we were selling the book, that line basically kicked open the door of every publisher we aimed it at. For some, the books and character were too challenging, but whether or not publishers liked the book, they couldn't ignore it. You have to find *some* stand-out quality in your tale, or readers/agents/editors won't be interested.

Oh, and the stand-out ingredient has to be genuinely enticing. 'The first police procedural set in Loughborough' or 'the first teen romance to be set in North-Western Arkansas' won't cut it. And just adding the wrinkles that all authors chuck into their books won't save a lousy idea. So if you want a hard-drinking maverick cop with a some dark issues in his past – well, you can have one, but those things won't separate you from the herd.

Write well

If you don't write well, nothing will work for you. Yes, the better the concept, the worse your execution can be. But really, you need a good idea AND a strong execution. (And yes, *Fifty Shades*. And OK, Dan Brown. But still. Please. Good writing.)

Know your genre

A big one, this, and really important. Unless you know your genre as a reader, you won't really know what stands out and what doesn't. Suppose for example, you had only the sketchiest acquaintance with modern crime writing and suddenly thought, 'Hey, I know, wouldn't it be cooool if I had a forensic scientist at the heart of an investigation.' And yes. Damn right. That would be cool … if this were 1990. But it isn't. So that idea, on its own, is of zero value, zero interest.

When I first got into crime writing, I knew my recent acquaintance with the genre wasn't strong enough, so I bought twenty books by twenty contemporary crime authors, read the lot, and bunged the results in a spreadsheet. (Police procedural versus private investigator. Series versus standalone. First person versus third person. Male protagonist versus female. And so on.) I didn't let that spreadsheet tell me what to write, but the ideas that I came up with – and that I love – bubbled up from a real engagement with the market as it was.

So that's it.

For Alessandro: *write from the heart*.
For Zachary: *write for the market*.

Do both things always, write well and be happy. Easy.

Harry

PS: Got something to tell me? Well, I am a human and … oh heck, you know the drill.

PPS: Want to know the major types of Publishing Car Crash? Are you all at sea trying to figure out your book's genre? Good job we've been busy on YouTube then:

Publishing car crashes and how to avoid them.
What genre is your book?.

PPPS: Recently received in our Agony Aunt corner:

'Dear Harry, I am frustrated and upset at not being able to book tickets RIGHT NOW for your genuinely amazing Festival of Writing 2019. Can you please tell me that bookings will open really soon? Yours, Impatient of Ipswich.'

'Dear Impatient of Ipswich. Yes. Bookings will open soon. Relax. Yours, Harry.'

(More marketing gold. Blimey, I'm good.)

PPPPS: Hate writing? Appalled by this week's lack of proper promotional PSs? Build a ship in a bottle and have done with these damn emails.

Interesting. But why the cannibalism?

I saw my agent yesterday. Because I do so much more with self-publishing these days, and because I've been so busy with Jericho Writers, I've talked to him less over recent months than I usually would, and it was a pleasure to sit and drink coffee and talk books.

Now, I may have some further titbits from that session in later emails, but there's one thought in particular I'd like to work with today.

Although I'm busily at work on Fiona Griffiths #7 at the moment, I do have a couple of other passion projects that I'd like to bring to fruition at some point. One of these is a very quirky, literary idea, with the provisional title of *The Most Excellent And Lamentable True Historie Of The Sailor, Gregorius*. (Interesting fact: if that book ever sees the light of day, it'll be my second book to have a comma in the title.)

The book's denouement involves a wee spot of cannibalism and I mentioned this fact to my agent.

Now, because the project is very quirky, and because the book is extremely short, it may or may not sell. It would actually be OK with me if it doesn't find a buyer – I wrote the thing for fun, and never originally intended publication. But if it does sell, it would need to sell as a *literary* project: something with depth. Something with a meaningful and resonant theme.

So yes, my agent wanted to understand what the book was. How it worked. How it was going to make sense of its Big Idea. But the next thing he said was, 'Interesting. But why the cannibalism? What's that a metaphor *for*?'

And I was taken aback by the question. First, because it's not something anyone has ever asked about one of my crime novels. Second, by the assumption that it was a metaphor *for* anything. And third – mostly – because I didn't have an instant answer.

A few thoughts about all this.

First, if you're writing literary fiction, you need to be able to answer questions about theme and metaphor and all that. That's how you prove your book is a proper literary novel, not just a nicely written and interesting book.

So when you write your agent query letter, talk about those themes. Say this kind of thing: 'The theme of silence haunts the book – and in particular the way silences can be enriching and fertile. I came to write the book, indeed, after spending six months alone in the wilderness of [the Canadian Rockies/a Tibetan monastery/a studio apartment in Poughkeepsie].'

I generally advise that a query letter should be no more than a single page of text, but there are two exceptions. Non-fiction authors may just need more space to set out their stall. And literary authors have to allow for an extra two paragraphs of yadda about themes and all that. You can't neglect it. It's a selling point.

Second, I personally tend to approach themes very obliquely. I tend to think that all well-written and complex works of fiction will find themselves addressing big issues in a subtle yet forceful way. It's like they can't help themselves: as though the human brain just *will* project meaning onto any large and carefully textured canvas.

One example: I once wrote a book (*Glory Boys*) about aviation and Prohibition, set in 1920s America. At one level, the book was just a straightforward adventure romp. That's why its readers bought it. At the same time, themes just crept in. As well as just the adventure stuff, the book came to be about the father-son relationship, and heroism, and the different sorts of heroism that could exist.

I would never have talked about those things when I was starting the book, or even have spent much time thinking about them. But as I was editing the book into shape and saw those themes emerging, I did a little to help them on their way. To clarify them for the reader. I've tended to think that too direct an approach risks making things a bit crass. A bit on-the-nose.

As a writing technique, maybe that's OK. As a sales technique – and especially as a sales technique for literary work – that's definitely not OK. So think:

'what is this book about at a deep level? What bigger themes are moving under the surface?'

The third point I want to make is that even if your book is a commercial rom-com, or a straightforward police procedural, or anything else, your book probably does have and should have some big themes swimming around. Think, for example, of *Breaking Bad*, the TV show. Yes, it's a show about the illegal drugs trade, but it's also about a man's descent into evil. About his partner's emergence into something like goodness and humanity. About the varying reactions of others to that evil, and the money it generates.

That was a massive and totally commercial show, all right, but it knew damn well it had some big themes. (The central character's name? Walter White – a massive clue that the show knew it was taking an innocent 'clean' character and dirtying him up.)

And last – I don't care how commercial your work is. The simple fact is that books with depth outsell ones without. Yes, there are exceptions (hello, James Patterson!), but not all that many. Themes make a book more memorable. They echo for longer in the memory. And that echo is what means a reader is more likely to reach for your second book, and your third, and your fourth. It'll make them more likely to post an Amazon review, or talk about your book to their friends.

Themes sell. Meaning sells. Depth sells. Don't discount those things, just because you're writing in a commercial genre.

Which brings me back to my agent's question: why the hell was I writing about cannibalism? Why *that*?

And on the train back from London, I thought more about that question and my rather rubbish answer. And I realised that, indeed, there was a precise and accurate reason why cannibalism featured. Because my strange tale of Gregorius the Sailor is most of all a book about story itself. The way stories feed off one another. The way stories become a part of our deepest being.

And that's cannibalism. A cannibal eats the flesh of another human, but then that other human becomes a part of the cannibal. For ever. Just as we're a composite of all the things we've ever eaten, we're also a composite of all the stories we've ever heard, and all those stories have fed off a million other stories. And so on.

So I emailed my agent and explained myself better, and he liked the explanation. Whether he likes the book … well, that's another matter completely. We'll just have to see. I do now kinda hope Gregorius gets to set sail on his adventures, but he's already done so in my head, which is where it matters most.

Till soon.

Harry

PS: Got something to tell me? Well, I am a human and ... oh heck, you know the drill.

PPS: Hate writing? Still working on your Genius Brexit Plan? Unsubscribe to these emails now and get cracking. It's the 29th of March, and time's a-running out.

When supermarkets rule ...

I mentioned last week that I'd have some more titbits from my recent agent chat – and, sure enough, that's all coming up.

First, though, as you probably know, we've just launched our Festival of Writing, so I thought I'd say something about what the Festival is and who it is/isn't right for.

[Editor's note: Harry is talking here about Jericho Writers' own annual Festival, but because what he says is applicable to almost any major writers' conference, we've kept his comments intact, in the hope that they're of value to you.]

Before that, however, a confession:

When we were preparing to run our first Festival, I kept struggling with two feelings. One was sheer anxiety: would anyone come? Would we be able to get agents and other industry pros to the event? Would the whole thing be a rank disaster?

Since the Festival costs an absolute minimum of £50,000/$80,000 to put on (and, in practice, a good bit more than that), I was frankly terrified. If we didn't sell enough tickets, I'd make a huge loss, and that would not have been a great conversation round the marital dinner table.

The second feeling, though, was simply: did anyone actually *need* the Festival? We'd always told clients (and still do) that agents' slush piles represent THE front door into the traditional industry. It was just fine to send your stuff off to an agent with whom you had absolutely zero previous contact – and if your book was good enough, it would be taken on.

That was true then. It's still true now. So why the Festival?

And I still don't really have an answer to that question. I'm no longer unsure about the basic quality of the event. On the contrary: a kind of magic happens there, and it happens reliably every year and to a zillion different types of author too.

But why? What's special? What's the magical ingredient?

And that's where I fall a bit short. The main thing, I think, is the synchronicity of everything. So you might go to a plotting workshop in the morning, have an agent one-to-one in the afternoon, have a brilliant conversation with a fellow writer at dinner – and something similar all the next day too – and the result is just more than the sum of its parts. It's not simply that you come away with a solution to the plot niggle in part two. It's not just that you made real contact with an agent, who is encouraging you to follow up. It's that you've changed. You've become a different, more capable, more confident writer.

There's stardust too. So let's say your novel is really good and ready for launch. If you stand up in front of a 300+ audience on Friday night and read your work out and people love it – well, magic happens. The first person to have won that Friday Night Live competition left the Festival with seven agents wanting to represent her, then went on to experience a highly contested auction ... and ended up having a major bestseller.

Would that outcome have happened without the Festival? Well, yes, it could have done. But no question, the Festival adds an ingredient there, a buzz of excitement, that rippled right on through the publishing process before splashing to shore on the bestseller lists. That buzz is the thing that the industry always craves, that it fights to achieve and usually can't. Well, the Festival can and routinely does. It's a bit of magic on the magic.

So who should come to the Festival? Who shouldn't?

Well, let's deal first with those who probably shouldn't. The Festival probably isn't right for you if you write non-fiction (with the exception of narrative non-fiction). If you write only short stories or flash fiction or poetry, it probably isn't right for you either. If you are already properly published or confidently self-publishing, you may not have a lot to learn there either.

If you are really only just starting out with your writing, then the Festival *might* be for you – just be aware that you'll be in the company of writers who are mostly more experienced than you. If you think that'll be intimidating, then avoid the Festival this year, and come next year instead. If you think that'll be inspiring, you should certainly come. The Festival has a really warm and inclusive atmosphere, so you shouldn't experience anything other than positivity and encouragement.

As for who *should* come – well, I think the Festival should suit anyone with a full-length novel, either written or well underway, who has a serious intention to seek traditional publication. I can't imagine being that writer and not getting a lot from the Festival. After all, the entire thing is designed around you, and your needs and your questions and the ingredients that we know will help you grow.

If you are just such a writer, we'd LOVE to see you there. Every single year, the Festival is my favourite weekend. And it's because of you guys. The enthusiasm, the belief, the warmth, the community. I love it!

(Oh, and we're no longer terrified of making a loss! We don't, in fact, generate huge profits from the event, but at least we know the damn thing won't bankrupt us. Phew!)

Right. Enough of that.

Agents. The market. What do publishers want?

And I think the answer can be summed up in three broad generalisations.

First, this is a great time for intelligent, broad spectrum non-fiction. So if you're a neurologist with interesting material on (say) memory, or creativity, or nature/nurture, or love, then there's a publisher who wants your book. Equally, there'll be publishers who want books on current affairs, on history, on politics, on science, and on much else.

The big challenge for such writers is writing a genuinely popular book. That is, you need to take relatively technical academic research and present it in a way that genuinely engages a broad (but intelligent) audience. The go-to author for this kind of writing is Malcolm Gladwell. He delivers real intelligence, with the grip of a thriller. That's the aim.

If you're deeply interested in a given non-fiction topic, but don't have natural authority (that is: you aren't an academic or other qualified professional), you don't have to give up. I'm not a historian – didn't even study the topic at university – but it's something that has always interested me. So I wrote a book of popular history. I wasn't going to be able to use my great academic record to launch the work, so I had to rely on just writing damn well. Making the book funny, interesting, engaging. Publishers didn't even really ask me whether I knew my stuff – they just believed me – and they liked the text. So after an intensely contested auction, I sold that book for more cash than anything else I've ever written. If we were selling it today, we might even make more.

That's one generalisation about what publishers want today. The second one is this:

This is a great time to write big, high-concept standalone books. That sort of sounds obvious, but it's a little less obvious than it sounds. In the old days, when bookstores sold more, and the supermarkets sold less, publishers really wanted the kind of writer they could turn into a series. So police procedural authors (like Michael Connelly or Ian Rankin) were really hot. By buying and establishing a great first-in-series book, publishers could make great money for dozens of books thereafter.

These days, supermarkets increasingly dominate the way publishers think about the world, and supermarkets are a terrible place to launch and sustain any kind of series fiction. Yes, supermarkets might buy a ton of your terrific book #1, but there'll be nothing in them that makes them think, 'Better stock book #2 when it comes out, otherwise we'll be letting down our customers.' They need to keep books on the shelves, same as they need to keep beans on the shelves, but they aren't there to provide a rounded book-purchasing experience. And they don't care either: their customers come for the beans and might buy a book. Of the two, the beans matter more.

So standalones do well. And given that supermarkets are selling to not-very-committed readers, you really want a standalone with a concept that drives sales from the title, cover and shoutline alone. Sure, you need to deliver good back-of-book blurb as well. But the actual text? It just matters less to this kind of purchasing decision. Think of your own habits. In a bookstore or on Amazon, you may well browse a few pages before buying a book. In a supermarket, that just feels out of place. If the price is right, and the jacket looks great, you pop the book in your basket, and go on to pick up the beans.

That means, you really need to work your elevator pitch hard. If you want some examples of great shoutlines, then how about:

I Let You Go, by Clare Mackintosh:
A tragic accident. It all happened so quickly. She couldn't have prevented it. Could she?

The front cover made a big deal about the mid-book twist, so buyers knew (a) the basic set-up for the story, and (b) that there was a big twist in store. That, plus a tear-jerky title and a brilliant cover, proved to be marketing gold.

Her Last Tomorrow, by Adam Croft:
Could you murder your wife to save your daughter?

This is a brilliantly marketed self-pub book – but that tagline could have sold the book in shedloads on any platform at all. It's a model of how to do it.

For what it's worth as well, the standalone geopolitical thriller has made a big comeback, after long years in the wilderness. Thank Trump, Putin, Xi and Brexit for that.

The third generalisation is that literary fiction has become increasingly tough to place in Big Five firms (because the sales just aren't there). But the flipside of this is that there's an increasingly vibrant and exciting micro-publisher world for difficult, interesting, challenging literary work. So if you're writing something of that sort, you may not get the deal with Penguin that you always wanted … but the indie publisher options are better now than they've been for decades.

That's it from me. Sorry about the length of this email. I've given you some incredibly meagre PSs by way of apology.

Till soon.

Harry

PS: Got something to tell me? Well, I am a human and … oh heck, you know the drill.

PPS: Hate writing? Want to make the world's most over-the-top Easter Bonnet? Unsubscribe to these emails now. They'll only distract you.

Pen-y-cwm – the end of the valley

Today we're doing my favourite thing. We're talking about writing.

And, you know what? I told myself yesterday that today we'd do something wholesome like talking about points of view and how to handle multiple protagonists. But now that I'm actually at the laptop, I don't want to do that at all.

Instead: I want to talk about something that I have a real passion for and is, I think, one of the things that I do well as a writer. That thing is turning place into character and using place as a whole extra (and brilliantly enjoyable) layer of storytelling.

And here's the thing: it's easy to let place drift to the bottom of your novel-writing priorities. Often the issue is a combination of factors. One, you've got a lot to think about and place doesn't often leap to the top of the list. Two, maybe you're dealing with places that seem very familiar to you, and it's hard to see your readers wanting to hear about them too much. Three, if you do make mention of place, your first attempts at those descriptions seem a little bland, so you end up chopping that text out in the edits.

Well, yes: I've made those errors myself. But oh, my friend, do not be lured away by the Place Doesn't Matter demons. They are temptresses and their gift is wailing (and rejection letters).

If you're still tempted by those demons, just think about why we read in the first place. Yes, we want to read a story, but in particular we want to experience story through the eyes of one or more central characters. And if that story is to engage our emotions, *it needs to feel real.* The experience of your main character in their fictional world needs to feel as believable as your own experience of the world.

In other words: if your novel doesn't have a credible and compelling sense of place, your reader will feel that little bit removed from your character – and your story has just lost power. Quite unnecessarily too.

That's the why. The how is simple too.

You need to:

Say something descriptive about your setting fairly early on in a scene. You're talking, probably, about a couple of sentences.

Keep nudging at that description as you go through the scene. A sentence here, a phrase there. Anything to keep the action physically anchored in your location.

How much description? Well, you need to play this by ear, really. If you're in a complex and exotic location, which impinges strongly on your character, you'll need more than two sentences to start off with, and the nudges will be more frequent and more insistent. If, on the other hand, you're in a location you've used a lot before, you'll tend to be fairly brief (and probably allude to any observable *changes* to the setting: 'The canteen was empty now, or almost. A couple of uniformed officers were drinking coffee and …')

That's kinda obvious and boring, but it gets more interesting:

As a human, you need physical data to help you navigate the world without bumping into things, but that physical data doesn't particularly engage your emotions. So when you're writing, your task is not to supply anything much in terms of useful physical data. Rather, your task is to pick out those elements of the location that will engage your point-of-view character at an emotional/visceral level.

And once you've grasped that point, then it starts getting quite exciting – because what emotional elements of a location do you want to bring out? The answer there, is that the location itself is almost certainly neutral. But your story/scene isn't neutral. Your character isn't neutral. So the thing that gives your location its atmosphere will be whatever *quality in that place most reverberates with the emotional action* of the story.

Exciting, right? And there are two broad ways you can go. You can have locations that are complementary to the action (a proposal scene in a rose garden, say.) Or you can have ones that clash or reverberate interestingly with the action. (For example, you set that romantic proposal scene in a multi-storey carpark when it's kicking down with rain.)

Now, there's quite a lot more to be said here. So next week, I think it would be fun to pick this up again. Oh yes, and right down at the bottom of the PSs, I've shoved a chunk of text from my book, *This Thing of Darkness*. The scene is set on a fishing trawler in the East Atlantic. My cop, Fiona Griffiths, is there undercover as a cleaner/cook. The sea is rising. There's all manner of naughty stuff about to happen. And the scene below has absolutely no story-relevance at all. It's just a way to get that place, that environment as alive and vivid as possible before the denouement finally denoues.

Have fun. Write well. See you soon.

Harry

PS: Got something to tell me? Well, I am a human and … oh heck, you know the drill.

PPS: Hate writing? Why not farm carp instead? Meantime, unsubscribe to these emails. They are seldom carp-related.

PPPS: Here's that chunk of text I mentioned. There's a kind of madness present in this scene and, though no violence takes place, you can feel the possibility of it at every movement. Look at the nouns I use too – guts, slime, eel, python, muscle, clatter, pumps, compressors, assault, seaspray, and so on. Nouns are an incredibly emphatic way to bolt down a sense of place. It's a pretty reliable rule, in fact: if the nouns are interesting, the description is too. And if they're not, it isn't. With a little luck, and even stripped of context, this scene will make you feel (a bit) as though you're actually there.

Here goes:

The room [where the fish are processed] *is awash. With sea water tramped in from outside. With the fresh water used to clean blood from the gutted fish. With guts and slime.*

I use a plastic broom to sweep the mess into a corner. Try to slide a shovel under the slippery pile before the moving deck heaves it aside and away from my bucket, a thing the size of a laundry-basket. One time, the pile includes an eel – or something like that, a sea serpent, I want to say, a python of the deep – and the damn thing evades my shovel every time I try to lift it. Slithering away as if still alive. A six-foot cord of black and glistening muscle, ending in a mouth large enough to swallow itself.

Buys and Coxsey are on processing duty, and Buys watches my efforts with a bloodshot eye.

He says nothing. The ship is, in any event, by now so noisy – with the engines, the clatter of processing machinery, the pumps and compressors, the unceasing assault of waves against the hull – that we don't talk except when we need to. And when we need to, we shout, mouth to ear. Gestures big, emphatic and repeated. Swearwords falling like seaspray.

Another attempt with the shovel, another failure.

I've been awake twenty-one hours now – Honnold gave me three hours off, but I couldn't sleep, couldn't even lie down really – and I don't know what to do. Don't know how to get the fucking eel into the fucking bucket. Keep trying, keep failing, as the ship bucks and the greenish light clots the air.

Buys drops his filleting knife. Those things are so fearsomely sharp that they snick through a fish as long as a man's forearm with only a whisper of effort. The knife rattles around the steel fish tray, as though in search of its next victim.

Buys approaches. Demented as I am, as he is, I think, He's going to hit me. I can't get the eel into the bucket and Jonah Buys is going to hit me. *I sort of accept it, too. There's an internal logic in my head which says,* That's only fair. Your job was to get the eel in the bucket and you were given a fair old try at it. You've no reason to complain.

But Buys doesn't hit me. Just takes the shovel from my hand, and with three or four smashing blows splits the eel into rags. Doesn't divide it cleanly, by any means, but leaves the thing in a series of bloody stumps, connected by tatters of skin and the white threads of exposed nerves.

Buys fixes me with that bloodshot eye, nods, goes back to his knifework. My shovel has no prob-

lem now heaving the mass into my bucket. It feels as though the world has become more orderly. Ah yes, that's how you clean a room. You smash any once-living creature into fist- and foot-sized fragments, then just shovel it away. *I carry my bucket over to the trash chute, where our discards go, and send the eel, and all its fishy co-travellers, to the next stop on their black roads.*

How to write a scene

So: stories are made of scenes strung together in a plot. Let's just assume for now that your plot is OK. In which case, the quality of your book is going to hang, to a very large extent, on the quality of your scenes. What makes a scene work? What are the tricks of the trade? What are the things you need to look out for?

Well, the curious little secret is that these things are (mostly) obvious and simple. They're just hard to do. So, here are some rules:

- Jump to the action as fast as you can
- If you want, you can jump right into the action, even at the cost of not quite making sense initially. You can then, 2-3 paragraphs in, go and back-fill the information the reader needs to make sense of things. So, for example, you might start with dialogue, without the reader knowing where the characters are situated. Once you've got things going via dialogue, you can add the, "They were standing in the middle of a …, etc". That often

gives you a stronger more engaging start, than starting with a description could ever deliver.
- Leave the scene as fast as you can. You can always tie up any loose threads in the next scene … and you probably need to tie fewer things up than you might think.
- It's often said that every scene needs to have a kind of conflict. I don't think that's quite right – or at least, it's not the most helpful way of describing things. What IS true is that there needs to be something unsettled in the scene. Something mobile. A question that needs an answer.
- Your character's emotions need to be engaged. If he/she doesn't care, your reader won't care.
- In general, but not always-always, you want a balance of scene description (so your scene is physically realised), dialogue (because that's the most supple, alive element in any scene) and action (in the sense that we know what your characters are doing.)
- There should for preference be a useful reverberation between the action that's taking place and the physical atmosphere in the scene. That can be obvious (a proposal in a rose garden) or contrasting (a proposal in a butcher's shop), but you want some alive, interesting echo between action and place.

- And here's a biggie: you structure your scenes much as you structure a story. You set up the question early on in the scene. You develop it. You reach a climax. You resolve quickly and move on.

Now all that seems pretty wholesome. A good, wholegrain style menu for writing a scene. But because that kind of advice seems pretty damn bland taken on its own, here's a mini-scene of my own, with my comments in brackets added.

The situation here is that my character, Fiona, has just escaped from a damaging and traumatising situation. She has fled to a buddy of hers: a guy called Lev, who is ex-Russian Special Forces and not exactly a run-of-the-mill character. She trusts Lev to look after her, but Lev needs to find his range first. Here's how things go:

> *I park where Lev tells me to, outside a cream-painted house, with a sheet of graffitied chipboard for a door.* [HB note: Very swift intro to the physical location. So brief, it hardly interrupts things.]
>
> *'Is here,' says Lev.*
>
> *The door is held by a crude wooden catch. No lock.* [HB note: Fiona's observing this. By noticing the crudity of the accommodation, she is letting you know, in effect, what she's thinking.]

Lev opens the door for me — there are no hinges, so he has to lift it — and I step inside.

I knew that Lev didn't have a permanent home in Britain or, I think, anywhere. Mostly he sleeps in his car or on the floors of friends' houses. But when he isn't doing those things, and isn't abroad, he uses squats.

But knowing that and being here: two different things. [HB note: Again, Fiona isn't saying, "I feel X about this place." But she's letting us know all the same. Indirect access to character emotions is just fine.]

The downstairs room is lightless. The doors and windows have been boarded up front and rear. There's a poor-quality kitchen in place — white formica doors loose on their hinges, chipboard surfaces bubbling and splitting with damp — but I already know there's no water in the tap, no power in the sockets. [HB note: More physical description. But this isn't done for its own sake. By now, it's clear that the question raised by this scene is roughly: "Is this horrible squat going to satisfy Fiona's needs for sanctuary? And how will her discomfort shift her relationship with Lev?" Those aren't huge questions in the context of the story. But they don't have to be. They just have to feel alive and important for the duration of a (shortish) scene.]

Lev says nothing. Just points me upstairs.

Upstairs: two bedrooms, one bathroom, nothing else. Bare boards. No furniture. No heating. No bathroom fittings, even. Lev has taken over the larger of the two bedrooms. A military looking roll of bedding, neatly furled. A ten-litre jerry can of water. A wash bowl. A primus stove and basic cooking equipment, all clean, all tidy. A black bag, of clothes I presume. A small box of food. The front window was boarded, but Lev has removed the boards and they stand leaning against the wall. [HB note: This is the first revelation of the accommodation proper. In that sense, what's gone before has been just preamble. This is where the scene-question gets sharpened up further.]

Light enters the room in silence. Leaves again the same way.

I don't say anything.

Don't even step into the room, not really. Just stand there in the doorway. [HB note: So, everything's hanging. At the moment, we're reaching a moment of crisis in our mini-story. Will this squat work for Fiona? It's not looking good. Her hanging back in the doorway (rather than stepping forward into the room) is as close as she gets to actual conflict with Lev. And that's not much conflict. That's why I don't think focusing on conflict is especially helpful.]

I am not what you would call a girly girl. I don't have a particular relationship with pink. Don't revere handbags or hoard shoes. I don't love to dress up, or bake, or follow faddy diets, or learn new ways to decorate my home. On the other hand, I have just spent the weekend being tortured in a barn near Rhayader and I was, I admit it, wanting something a bit homelier than this. [HB note: Fiona humour! And for the first time really direct access to her thoughts / feelings. Again, this is pushing us closer to the point of crisis/decision/resolution.]

Lev stands behind me seeing the room through my eyes. Perhaps he was secretly expecting me to be thrilled. Perhaps he is thinking dark thoughts about decadent Western girls, our need for luxury. [HB note: More humour. But here we have Lev's position and Fiona's. At the moment, these are two opposed, unresolved forces. We don't yet know how this is going to resolve.]

He says nothing. Not straight away. We just stand there in the pale light. Even the tiniest sounds echo among these hard surfaces, so a single creak of a floorboard rolls around the room, like a pea in a shoebox. [HB note: Tension ratchets up for a couple of lines. Then ...]

Then Lev says, 'Is not suitable.'

That was halfway between a question and a statement, but I let it be a statement.

Lev says, 'We go somewhere else.' [HB note: Boom! Done. We know that Fiona's opposition has won the day. As far as we can tell at this stage, the Fiona / Lev relationship hasn't been injured by that micro-conflict. And of course a new story question is immediately launched: Lev still seems willing to find sanctuary for Fiona, but what is he going to offer? Will Fiona find her sanctuary? And will that be enough to allow for her recovery? Those questions are immediately tackled by the scenes that follow.]

That's it. As you can see, not a lot of heavy-duty story-freight hangs on that scene. In a way, you could cut it completely and the book would lose nothing much in terms of plot. But from the reader's perspective, the scene is funny. It's tense. And they learn something about Lev (the way he lives) that they may have been curious about for the space of about 400,000 words (i.e. since the moment they first met him in book #1 of the series.)

And one other thing: the scene is short. That whole thing notches up just 450 words, or about a page and a half of a paperback. But that's still long enough to launch a question, develop it, build some tension round it, have plenty of personality / emotion / humour in the situation, then resolve it and move on. Do that enough times in the course of a properly plotted story, and you have a book, my friend.

Happy New Year.

Harry

PS: Let's have a chit chat on Townhouse. If you haven't signed up yet, then please do.

PPS: Hate writing? Want to go and live in a squat? Be my guest, but unsubscribe right now, if you don't mind.

All about editing

This week I was going to plunge into more descriptions of place, but now I'm actually at the keyboard, I realise I want to write about something else. The something else is inspired by a blog post I've just written which talks about the incredibly confusing world of third-party editing. So, to list just some of the terms you hear kicking around, you can go out and buy yourself:

- Developmental editing.
- Structural editing.
- Substantive editing.
- Manuscript assessment (or editorial assessment).
- Line editing.
- Copyediting.
- Proofreading.

And then – not really editing, but still in the same broad ballpark – you can go and get yourself:

- Fact-checking.
- Indexing.

- Formatting (for e-book).
- Typesetting/internal layout design (for print).

All that can seem pretty overwhelming. Are you meant to do *all* those things? Or only some – in which case, which ones, and in which order?

Yikes.

OK, so let's start simple.

If you are heading for traditional publication, you don't *need* to do any of those things, ever, at any stage. When I got my first novel published, I edited my work damn hard by myself, then got an agent, then got a publisher, and the publisher took care of the rest.

Yes, that was a while ago, but the same basic approach still works perfectly fine today. (Just one little caveat: your book has to be very good if it's going to get the agent and the publisher on board. I'll come back to that point in a moment.)

If you're heading for self-publication, then clearly no publisher is going to step up and take care of the production process for you, so you're going to have to do it yourself. But the only stages that really demand your attention are these:

- Some kind of structural editing (to get your story as good as it can be).
- Some kind of copyediting (to make sure that the text is reasonably free of typos and the like).
- Formatting (for e-book).

- Internal layout design (for print).

These days, you can take care of those last two stages automatically, just by uploading a Word document to Amazon. Better practice is to master the tools of your trade yourself, or to use some cheap-but-good formatting place, like bbebooksthailand.com. That just leaves two basic processes to worry about (getting the story right, getting the text right). These days, both processes are essential. As the self-pub market has matured and professionalised, readers now simply reject any book that isn't properly presented.

At this point in the email, I ought to say something like this:

'Did you know Jericho Writers offers top quality copyediting?'

So OK. Yes. We offer top quality copyediting at competitive prices.

Thing is though, I don't actually think you should buy copyediting. Not even ours. (Sorry, everyone in our marketing department.)

How come?

Well, if you're heading for trad-land, then a publisher will take care of copyedits for free. If you're heading for Planet Indie, then you should aim to cut costs wherever possible, and copyediting is probably a task you can hand over to any really picky, eagle-eyed friend of yours. (Or, ideally, bunch of friends. Amateurs, even gifted ones, will miss a lot of issues.)

And sure, your manuscript will be that little bit less clean and perfect than it would be if you used a pro. But so what? You're starting out. You can get more professional once you're generating some decent income.

So for indies, the 'what kind of editing?' question comes back to the issue of how best to improve your novel itself – the story, the pacing, the characters, the everything.

And that, unsurprisingly, is the one that faces traditionally orientated writers too. It's all very well to say that a publisher will be able to supply all the various editorial elements for free, but how do you get the agent and the publisher in the first place?

Egg, meet chicken.

Chicken, meet egg.

So let's say that you know you want to improve your manuscript and you're getting close to the point where your self-editing efforts are running out of steam. What then? What do you do next?

Well, despite what seems like a plethora of editing options, there are really only two. They are:

Developmental editing – that is, someone actually goes in and cleans up your manuscript for you.

Structural editing – in other words, someone advises you on where the problems are and what to do about them. The actual hands-on solution of those problems remains your task, however.

Needless to say, developmental editing is more expensive, which means it's more lucrative, which means people like me should be telling you to buy lots of it.

Except (sorry again, marketing people) I don't think you should – or at least you should seriously pause before taking that step.

The issues here are at least threefold.

First, developmental editing of the worst sort teaches nothing. With some of these services, you pop a problematic manuscript in at one end of a machine and get a cleaned-up version out the other end. So what? You've not built your skills at all, which means you'll have to go through the same painfully expensive process next time.

Second, you lose ownership of the book. Is it even your text anymore? Well, partially, perhaps – but who ever woke up in the morning and said, 'You know what? I want to partially write a book.'? That's never been an ambition of mine.

Third – and most important – if you pop a problematic and unpublishable manuscript into that kind of developmental process, you'll end up with a cleaned-up and *still unpublishable* manuscript. I have almost never seen a decent book emerge from that process, just because a great book needs to emerge from an author, not from some kind of semi-industrial process.

So me and the version of developmental editing where you just hand your book over to someone else? Yep. Well, we don't get on. I'll talk about exceptions in a moment or two.

That leaves the advisory-type editing. (Which you can call structural editing, or substantive editing, or editorial assessment, or – as we call it – manuscript assessment.) This works because you retain authorship of the book. Yes, you get an intelligent and experienced third party helping you navigate, but it's your book. Those are your problems and you'll be the one to solve them, albeit with a little guidance and advice.

And to be clear: I love this kind of editorial advice. Love it, love it, love it.

I've published about twenty books, depending on how you count, and every single one of them has had structural-type input before it's gone to print. And they've all got better. Every single one of them. It's almost magical.

At this point in the email, my very sad marketing people are starting to perk up, because I'm presumably about to start saying you should buy something – for example, our terrifically wonderful manuscript assessment services.

But (sorry again, marketing people), I think you probably *shouldn't* buy those services. Or not yet at least.

The way to get maximum value out of editorial feedback is to do as much self-editing work as you can yourselves first.

If you know there's a problem with Katerina's battle scene in part 2, then fix it. Or try to fix it. Do whatever you can to repair it.

Same thing with character niggles, or bland descriptions, or tedious dialogue, or whatever your other issues are. The more you handle those things yourself, the more you'll learn. Just as important, when you *do* get a pro assessment of your work, the editor will be identifying things that you hadn't seen at all or (more often) things you had seen but just didn't know how to fix.

Another too-long email again, so sorry about that. But to summarise:

You should avoid most paid-for sorts of editing, however problem-solving they look.

Manuscript assessments (advisory, structural editing) are absolutely brilliant. They're often real game-changers.

But don't rush into that kind of editing. Do as much as you can yourself. You'll learn more and get much better value if you self-edit hard before coming to us.

Oh yes. And I promised I'd tell you when developmental editing might work for you. It's where you (a) are already a fairly sophisticated writer, (b) can afford the not-insignificant cost, (c) get a proper manuscript assessment as part of the package, and (d) use the line-by-line edits as a way to deepen your understanding of craft at the sentence-by-sentence level. Yes, your manuscript will end up a lot cleaner than it was, but you'll also have the tools needed to complete any clean-up yourself ... and you'll have learned so much that you may not need the service at all with your next book.

And just to be clear: most writers don't check all those boxes, or don't yet. If in doubt, hold on to your pennies. They aren't always so easy to come by.

That all-about-editing article is available on the blog, if you're interested.

That's it from me. Now go out into a field and look at a baby lamb. They're pretty.

Harry

PS: I'm a human, you're a human, this is an email, and there is a reply button just waiting to be hit.

PPS: Hate writing? Love unsubscribing to things? Then unsubscribe to these emails. They're RUBBISH.

Editor's note:

As we were taking this book through the production process, we got it copyedited, of course. The copyeditor, Karen Atkinson, has had plenty of experience in working with self-pub authors and had this to say:

I would advise adding proofreading to the list of things that demand attention, especially if readers follow your advice to get friends and family to do the copyediting.

I've advised many self-pubbers that they can't expect a copyeditor to catch everything, especially when the copyedit is fairly heavy, and also that errors, including layout errors, may be introduced during typesetting.

I always encourage people to spend a lot more time self-editing (and suggest resources to help them do this) rather than parting them from a lot of cash for a heavy edit (which, as you point out elsewhere, they learn nothing from). I advise that if they are going to choose between copyediting and proofreading (rather than, ideally, purchasing both), their money is better spent on a final proofread of a well self-edited manuscript; the proofreader will check for both errors and layout issues. Some skip the self-editing step, get someone cheaper than me to copyedit, skip proofreading, and then come back and tell me I was right and that they are disappointed with the number of errors in the final version. They will have spent a lot of money on the whole thing anyway, but by skipping the final step, it's mostly wasted as they come out disappointed and with readers picking holes in it.

Our view? Yes, she's right. If you know your manuscript is very clean and with fairly few typos, you may get away with Harry's approach above. Or if your first self-pub book is intended to be a kind of low-cost toe in the water, then cutting costs also makes sense. But for anything else? Yes: you need to spend the money. These days, readers expect texts to look and feel properly professional.

A golden age

The market for traditionally marketed fiction is under pressure. I won't even reiterate those pressures here; I've banged on about them in the past, and will do so again in time to come. Suffice to say that Amazon isn't going to become less dominant. Self-publishers aren't going to curl up and go away. And supermarkets are not about to turn into book-supporting, culture-nurturing, publisher-loving behemoths.

But there's one area of the book market that always was strong, has grown still stronger, and looks set for still further growth.

In short, I want to talk a little about non-fiction, which is something these emails don't talk enough about. So we'll talk non-fiction in a second, but first, and with a tarantara, and a small but energetic parade made up of:

- a large but docile elephant;
- twelve dancers wearing ostrich feathers;
- a plump DJ dressed in a gold suit;
- a troupe of cold-looking children in fancy dress;
- a brass band from South Wales;

- somebody's dog –

It is my pleasure to announce that the Old Townhouse is dead. It has been blasted into a shower of binary, a fading wave of bits and bytes.

In its place – a new Townhouse. A Townhouse reborn.

This new Townhouse is an online community for writers – for people like you, in fact. It is completely free. It costs not a farthing, not a dime, not a sou, not a kopek.

It's a place where you can talk to others about writing. Where you can solicit critiques of your work. Where you can offer critiques in return. Where you can discuss the ins and outs of agents, publishers, self-pub, and everything else that lies beneath our inky sun.

Q: How do you gain access to this little wonderland?
A: You go to community.jerichowriters.com, my little dumpling, and hit 'Join us'.

Phew.
OK.
Non-fiction.

So: non-fiction is having something of a golden age. People seem to be reading more of it than ever before. There are various theories as to why this is, but my own answer is that non-fiction is the one area where Amazon and trad publishing form a kind of perfect marriage.

Trad publishing is brilliant at finding, nurturing and releasing books like Malcolm Gladwell's *Tipping Point*, or Kate Summerscale's *The Suspicions of Mr Whicher*, or Lars Mytting's weird hit *Norwegian Wood: Chopping, Stacking, and Drying Wood the Scandinavian Way*.

Self-publishers can't easily compete on that territory, because so many of the biggest non-fiction hits are one-offs, and self-pub marketing tactics all revolve around series promotions.

At the same time, bookstores can't easily stock all the non-fiction being published, because their shelves just aren't large enough.

But Amazon can.

And we readers can find whatever we want, whenever we want it, from Amazon. And while readers seem to like their fiction digital nowadays, we still have a preference for reading non-fiction in hard copy, so the market for 'online print' is far more buoyant in non-fiction than it is in fiction.

Long story short: trad publishers can go on producing beautiful non-fiction, Amazon can sell it, and we can read it. Everyone's happy. (And indeed, even indie bookstores are happy, because they can use Amazon as a kind of proving ground to see what's popular, then they can stock their shops with whatever works and watch it fly.)

What does that mean for you?

Well, I don't know, of course: I don't know what your passions are, or where your experience or knowledge lies. But here are some thoughts:

Professional experience

People love access to specialist and exotic worlds, especially if those worlds throw some interesting light on the one we live in. A perfect example of this would be Henry Marsh's *Do No Harm*, a collection of stories from Marsh's experience as a brain surgeon. That book did so well because you can't get a profession much more specialist and exotic than brain surgery – and yet the actual subject matter of the book rides the line where consciousness meets matter, a topic of universal interest and relevance.

As a recipe for a non-fiction hit, you can't really beat that.

The tiny thing that reveals a big one

Another brilliant formula for a non-fiction hit is to choose some object or type of thing, and see what happens when you view the world through that prism. A current hit of exactly this type is Anne Sverdrup-Thygeson's *Extraordinary Insects: Weird, Wonderful, Indispensable. The ones who run our world*. Another good example of the genre is *Gut*, by Giulia Enders.

I've happened to choose a couple of science-led subjects there, but you could equally well choose a city, or a theme from history, or a food ingredient, or anything that opens out to reveal a world bigger than you'd first imagined.

Novelistic approach

For all that we love non-fiction, the basic disciplines of story and vivid telling remain constant. If you have an interest in creative non-fiction, it's hardly an exaggeration to say that the skills you need are those of a novelist. Good writing sells.

Now yes, some of these books are frankly intimidating. Henry Marsh spent an entire career as a brain surgeon before writing his bestselling books on the subject. That's one heck of an apprenticeship, to put it mildly.

But the truth is, if you have a passion and *are a good writer*, you can write a book that sells. I wrote and sold a book of popular history (*This Little Britain*) without even having a history degree. I just like the subject I wrote about, and I wrote about it well enough to engage a publisher's enthusiasm.

The other huge advantage of non-fiction is that (oh joy!) you can sell the book before you've written it.

With *This Little Britain*, my agent and I made the sale off the back of about 10,000 words of actual text. That, plus an outline of the rest of the book. I hadn't actually researched the rest of the book, so my outline was wildly sketchy. But 4th Estate (my eventual publisher) didn't care. They just trusted me to get on with it.

If you want more non-fiction loveliness, then you can find a full account of how to put together a book proposal on the blog.

That's all from me. Now pluck some apple blossom and put it in a vase. I did that yesterday and how nice it looks.

Harry

PS: I'm a human, you're a human, so let's talk. But let's not talk by Smelly Old Email. Let's go to our brand new Townhouse and chat there.

I'll supply the mint tea. You bring the macaroons.

PPS: Hate writing? Prefer insects? Then unsubscribe to this email and go bug-hunting instead.

The days that say no

We start with a little admission:

I don't much want to write this email.

That's not usually true. Quite genuinely, writing this weekly email is usually one of my week's little highlights. I like writing it. I like sending it. I like the flow of conversation back again.

But today? I'm just feeling a bit low on energy. It's one of those days where I'd prefer just to sit outside with a good book. Or eat hot bacon with my fingers.

But there's something just a little sacred about this weekly email. It goes out bang on time every week. You expect it. I promise it. One wouldn't need to mess around with that basic contract very much before it started to get quite seriously frayed.

Hence I am writing this email. The bacon-with-fingers and book-read-outside bit will have to wait until this stern duty is performed.

But writing a book isn't quite like that. And it's not quite like that for two reasons.

A book's deadline is so floaty-out-there-in-the-void that a morning wasted feels neither here nor there. A matter of little consequence.

If you're not yet getting paid for your work, it's hard to claim that writing is a priority. Family stuff comes first. Work stuff comes second. And your poor old book, who'd like to be thought of as actual work, keeps finding itself at the bottom of the Dirty Laundry Basket of Life.

And those things are just plain realities. Nothing I say in this email will alter them much.

But, but, but …

The first thing I want to say is that guilt just isn't particularly helpful and writing books just is a creative business.

So if your day job is dry stone walling, and it happens to be raining on a workday, I'd say, 'Put your coat on and go build some wall. Stop moaning.'

If, however, your job is writing a book and your head just isn't in a place for that kind of intense creative activity, I'd always encourage you to try – for thirty or forty minutes perhaps – to see what comes. Sometimes that initial feeling of reluctance is nothing more than that feeling of getting ready to jump into cold water. Yes, it's a shock, but the shock soon fades and you start swimming.

But if, really truly, today just isn't a book-writing day, then it isn't. Either do the dishes or sit outside and read. Do whatever you and your body need. That's not something to feel guilty about. You are a human, not something built in a BMW factory. Sometimes we have off days, and that's OK.

That said, I do believe in goals and forward momentum. It's all very well to have a day off, but you do need a clock ticking somewhere. Your deadline needs to stay reasonably fixed, even if you have time off now and again.

But now we're driving down towards an issue that many of us will have felt.

Sometimes, it's not that today is an off day (which we're allowed), *it's that me and this book no longer seem to be getting along.*

Every day, the same problems. A love affair that seems to have disintegrated into a sad, messy, problematic relationship. You still remember the dreams that brought you here, but the dreams and the daily reality seem poles apart.

And here, I do have a useful insight to offer.

Assuming that you truly are a writer, assuming that you really do have the deep interior drive to play this game, then that day-after-day unhappiness with a book project means one of two things.

One, it can mean that your first draft is a first draft. And first drafts are a bit shite, so every day you are working with something that's not exactly smelling of roses.

The solution there is simple. Just keep on keeping on. In Jane Smiley's words: 'Every first draft is perfect, because all the first draft has to do is exist.'

In other words, you are a dry stone waller plying your craft on a wet January day. It might not be fun, but, stone by stone, you'll get there in the end.

That's one common issue, but the second one is perhaps just as common and a lot harder to self-identify. The issue is simply: *you have a technical problem with your current draft and you don't know what it is*.

You sort of know that this book isn't turning out right. So you add a chapter, or delete a chapter, or add some backstory, or delete a character, but the damn book still feels wrong. Maybe even wronger than when you started to mess with it.

And if that's your issue, the solution is simple:
Craft.

The more technical ability you have as a writer, the faster you diagnose and solve those issues. 'Heck, this isn't feeling right. It's not even feeling right for a first draft. What's going wrong? Oh, yeah. Too many points of view. I'll delete the two extraneous ones, patch over the joins, then move on. Yep, that should work. Bummer. I've wasted a bit of time, but at least I know what I'm doing next.'

That, very roughly (and minus a few inner expletives), is the internal thought process of the craft-competent writer.

Yes, you still make wrong turns, but you identify them more swiftly and correct them more adroitly.

Which is all very well for me to say – I've literally written books on the subject – but what about you? Where do you get that craft knowhow?

Well: anywhere, that's where.

Here are some of your options:

- **Just write more, battle longer.** That's a brilliant way to learn technique. The only absolutely essential one there is. It's the foundation for anything else.
- **Read books about how to write.** (Including this one!)
- **Take a course.**
- **Get editorial help.**

For me, the first two bullets on that list are easy, essential and cheap. Just do them. No excuses. Do them now.

Don't just buy and read one 'how-to' type book either. The more different perspectives you engage with, the more you'll start to formulate your own set of rules. The craft template that works for you.

If skills-building is what you're after, then I'd tend to think that taking a course was a better bet than getting an editorial review (which, I reckon, works best for late-stage writers.)

But actually, the real message of this email isn't that you should/shouldn't buy a particular course. It's that falling out of love with a book is often, maybe even usually, *the result of a specific, identifiable and fixable technical problem*. Once you know what the issue is, the fix is usually easy (though possibly a lot of work.)

And the result?

Relief.

Yes, you may go back to your draft aware that you need to rejig the plot or kill some points of view, *but you know what you are doing and why you are doing it.* The sense of stuckness just melts away into something much more like excitement.

That's when writing feels most alive, most vibrant. It begins with passion, but it endures through craft.

Happy writing. Happy editing. And now –
Bacon!

Harry

PS: We're all humans, and a really good place to find other writing-type humans is on Jericho Townhouse, our freer-than-free writers' community.

If you want to talk about the topics in this email, then let's do so on Townhouse. I'll engage fully with everyone responding on that thread. If you're not yet a Townhouse member, then sign up.

PPS: Fill in your own marketing idea here. Me, I've got nothing.

PPPS: Hate writing? Want to farm your own happy pigs on fields rich with black truffles and slippery with oak leaves? Then unsubscribe to this email now. THIS EMAIL TELLS YOU ABSOLUTELY NOTHING ABOUT PIG FARMING.

Let me count the ways

How many ways are there to get published?

In the old-old days, there was roughly one: you got an agent. That person got you a publisher. And *boom*, you did well. Or *fizzle*, you didn't.

Then, back in about 2011 or so, Amazon-led self-publishing became a thing. And since then, it's become an absolutely huge thing: a really effective way to sell books, find readers and earn a living.

But other routes have multiplied too.

What about traditional publishing but without an agent? What about APub, Amazon's own publishing house? What about Unbound and other crowd-funded routes to publication? What about Wattpad and all that?

And what about those snakes, those serpents, those venomous spiders of the vanity publishing world? Those guys too have multiplied and metamorphosed.

We realised, in fact, that our advice on all this was slightly out of date. So I ditched our old *Getting Published* article and wrote a monster one, which you can find on the blog.

I reckon there are at least twelve routes to publication, and I've listed them all, with pros and cons.

And because the simple topic of 'how to get published with traditional publisher via a literary agent' is in fact an exceptionally complex one, with lots of need-to-knows about what agents do, and how they do it, and how to find one, and how to write a synopsis, and all that stuff, we made sure that the blog post had links out to all the resources you could possibly need.

Because my fingers are shredded with the exhaustion of typing what may yet prove to be the Longest Blog Post ever, this email is a nice short one. Basically: if you want to know what routes to publication exist in 2020, then this blog post will tell you.

If you think I've left anything out – tell me.

If you disagree with anything I've said – tell me.

If you'd care to share that blog post on social media or on your blog, I'd raise my hat to you and offer you a half-pint of something with malt and hops in.

Till next week (when you'll get a PROPER EMAIL).

Harry

PS: We're all humans, and a really good place to find other writing-type humans is on Jericho Townhouse, our freer-than-free writers' community. Let's talk about this email there. Or just reply direct. I read everything I get and do always aim to reply.

PPS: Hate writing? Want to dress in goat skins and play the pan pipes? Then unsubscribe from these emails right now this minute.

The secret of style

Voice.

It's the secret sauce of writing. The magical herb that transforms your stew. It's the leaf of gold in a martini. The lemony brightness.

It's also, no surprise, the single thing that agents most often look for in a debut work. A *distinctive voice*. The key to success.

Although agents are most vocal in wanting this, I'd say that the same issue matters almost as much to self-published debuts. After all, if you're writing just another romance, the reader can buy any old romance to meet their needs. They don't have to buy your #2 in the series. But if you write something so distinctive that there's just no adequate substitute out there, they have to buy your #2, and then your #3, and then … No prizes for guessing which kind of self-pub author makes more money.

Right, so voice is good. But what is it? What actually are we talking about here?

Well, the dictionary definition would be something like: voice = the author's stylistic fingerprint. A distinctive way of writing, unique to that specific author.

Voice is most obviously applicable to questions of prose style. So Raymond Chandler's voice is immediately distinctive from the way he puts words on a page. This kind of thing from *Farewell, My Love*:

It was a blonde. A blonde to make a bishop kick a hole in a stained-glass window.

Or this, from *Red Wind*:

There was a desert wind blowing that night. It was one of those hot dry Santa Anas that come down through the mountain passes and curl your hair and make your nerves jump and your skin itch. On nights like that every booze party ends in a fight. Meek little wives feel the edge of the carving knife and study their husbands' necks. Anything can happen.

But voice has to do with more than just prose.

So if you think about (for example) *I Am Lucy Barton* by Elizabeth Strout, there's nothing so very remarkable about the way she puts words on a page. For example, this:

Then I understood I would never marry him. It's funny how one thing can make you realize something like that. One can be ready to give up the children one always wanted, one can be ready to withstand remarks about one's past, or one's clothes, but then – a tiny remark and the soul deflates and says: Oh.

That doesn't have anything like the showiness of Raymond Chandler. Each sentence is perfectly simple. The finish is rather flat, as though the author is painting in acrylics, not oils.

That sounds like a put-down. But the human/emotional insights are so precisely observed, so accurately and simply delivered, that their cumulative effect is overwhelming. The flatness of style is, in fact, closely married to the insight. The same kind of insight delivered in Chandler-ese would have deflected most of the attention to the writing and removed the power of the actual observation.

It's not hard to find voice in any author of real quality. Take Lee Child. He hardly operates at the literary end of the spectrum. You could slap a chunk of his prose down on the page and not find anything so remarkable. For example:

Never forgive, never forget. Do it once and do it right. You reap what you sow. Plans go to hell as soon as the first shot is fired. Protect and serve. Never off duty.

That doesn't look like authorial voice even a little bit. That looks like a chain of sentences lining up for the World Cliché Parade.

But – Jack Reacher. That's the secret of Lee Child's voice right there. The way Reacher thinks, acts, remembers, operates is a brilliant construct. Reacher certainly doesn't have any of Elizabeth Strout's quietly piercing observations, but Child gives us a complete, brilliant, detailed picture of the way a fighting machine like Reacher works. The (mostly) unremarkable prose is absolutely a part of that. Reacher doesn't do fancy, so the prose follows suit.

And, OK, all this is interesting. But we haven't yet said anything useful.

I mean, if voice is so important, then it would be kind of useful to know where to get it, how to build it.

And – I don't know.

Not really.

Or rather: I don't think there's a specific set of techniques you can use to go and get yourself a distinctive voice. In that sense, it's not like problems with prose, or problems with plot, where you can simply run a fairly standard set of diagnostic tools to identify the specific issues and find solutions.

On the other hand, I can tell you what kind of person you have to be to have voice. What kind of writer.

Above all, you have to be a confident one. Confident in yourself. I love quoting Gore Vidal on this. He says:

Style is knowing who you are, what you want to say and not giving a damn.

The hardest bit there is the *not giving a damn*. It's finding the mode of expression that works best for you, then just going for it. Taking off that inner handbrake. Following the logic of your path to its end. Ensuring, relentlessly, that you are satisfied with every last word on the page. That those words, in that order, spoken by those characters are what you want to express.

That means, in order to please an agent – you have to not give a damn about what an agent may think.

In order to please your eventual reader – you have to not care, or not care directly, about their judgements.

In effect, the finding-a-voice journey is an act of inner completion, that just happens to be executed via writing. Which is great. Which is uplifting. But which is also a real bummer, because what tools and techniques do you use to become a more complete human?

I don't really have a useful answer to that question. I'd say my voice was kinda present in my first ever novel – it didn't read exactly like anybody else's debut novel. But before I had anything like a completely confident voice, I'd written five (maybe six) novels and three or four works of non-fiction. And yes, I think there's something replicable about that technique. Write five or six novels that get published, and you'll find yourself writing in a Vidal-ish, not-giving-a-damn kind of way.

But some of you might be a little more impatient than that. And yes, as a voice-acquisition technique, I'd say my own process was hardly speedy.

So instead let me recommend these two approaches:

1. Learn writing technique

One of the reasons why newbie writers end up sounding undistinctive is that they have so much else to grapple with. Is my plot working? Should I choose first person or third? Does this character feel vivid? Does this relationship have enough conflict? (etc, etc, etc).

The result is that they never really get to grapple with those Gore Vidal-ish things at all. Their minds (and my mind, during those first few books of mine) are too pre-occupied with issues of mere technique.

So, lesson one, absorb writing technique until it's second nature. The more you absorb and internalise those tools, the more your mind is freed for other things. For self-expression and self-finding.

2. Rewrite

You can't be satisfied because something is OK. You can only afford to be satisfied when it is OK and expresses exactly what you wanted to say in the way that you wanted to say it.

And because you don't even know what you want to say until you start saying it, you'll find, almost inevitably, that you build your way towards something good by writing and unpicking, and then re-writing and re-unpicking, all the way until you're finally done.

That's lesson two.

3. Ignore anyone else's model

The next thriller writer to be as successful as Lee Child will not write like Lee Child.

The next crime writer to make as much of a mark as Raymond Chandler will definitely not write like Raymond Chandler (because zillions of people have written in a Chandler-lite kind of way and absolutely none of them made any kind of mark).

So forget about those models, great as they are.

Forget also about the endless peer-to-peer workshopping, practised by a lot of university creative writing programmes. That workshopping has plenty to be said for it, no doubt, but too much of it will turn your work into something that sounds like all those other creative writing MFA-type products. And you don't want that. You want to sound like you.

That's lesson three, and here endeth the lessons.

That's it from me.

I am now going to take a hayfever pill and declare war on every blade of grass in Oxfordshire.

Yours sneezily,
Harry

PS: This week, I'm going to put the whole text of this email up on Jericho Townhouse. I'll be happy to deal with comments and questions in the thread beneath. If you have an enquiry that's a bit more personal/private – then this is an email and I am a human. You know what to do next.

PPS: Hate writing? Want to murder any blade of grass that has the AUDACITY to try having sex in your nose? Then unsubscribe from these emails, and good luck, my friend.

Late nights and leakages

I had plans for today, plans that involved some interesting and actually useful work.

But –

Our boiler sprang a leak. Even with the mains water turned off, it went on leaking through the night. Finding an engineer who could come out today (for a non-insane price) took the first half hour this morning. The engineer is coming at 3.30, and that'll eat the last part of the day.

And –

I have a vast number of kids: four, in theory, but most days it seems like a lot more than that. And one of them, Lulu, spent most of the last couple of nights not very well at all.

So –

Not masses of sleep. And today's interesting work plans have been kicked into next week.

Which bring us to –

You. Life. Books. Writing.

The fact is that even if you're a pro author, life gets in the way of writing all the time. Because writing isn't an office-based job, almost no writer I know keeps completely clean boundaries between work stuff and life stuff. Life intrudes all the time. Indeed, I know one author – a multiple *Sunday Times* top ten bestseller – whose office-based partner always just assumes that she'll be the one to fix boilers, attend to puking children, etc, etc, just because she's at home and not under any immediate (today, next day) deadline pressure.

And that's a top ten bestseller we're talking about. Most of you aren't in that position. You're still looking for that first book deal. The first cheque that says, 'Hey, this is a job, not just a hobby.'

So Life vs Work?

Life is going to win, most of the time. And it'll win hands down.

The broken boiler version of life intrusion is only one form of the syndrome, though. There's one more specific to writers.

Here's the not-yet-pro-author version of the syndrome, in one of its many variants: you have one book out on submission with agents. You keep picking at it editorially and checking your emails 100 times a day. But you also have 20,000 words of book #2 on your computer and though, in theory, you have time to write, you're accomplishing nothing. You're just stuck.

It feels like only aspiring authors should suffer that kind of thing, right? But noooooooo! Pro authors get the same thing in a million different flavours, courtesy of their publishers. Your editor quits. Your new editor 'really wants to take a fresh look at your work, so as soon as she's back from holiday and has got a couple of big projects off her desk …'. Or your agent is just starting new contract negotiations with your editor, and you are hearing alarmingly little for some reason. Or you know that your rom-com career is on its last legs, so you're looking to migrate to domestic noir, but you don't know if your agent/editor/anyone is that keen on the stuff you now write. Or …

Well, there are a million ors, and it feels like in my career I've experienced most of them. The simple fact is that creative work is done best with a lack of significant distractions and no emotional angst embedded in the work itself. Yet the publishing merry-go-round seems intent on jamming as much angst in there as it can manage, compounded, very often, by sloppy, slow or just plain untruthful communications.

So the solution is …?

Um.

Uh.

I don't know. Sorry.

The fact is, these things are just hard and unavoidable. Priorities do get shifted. You can't avoid it. The emotional strains of being a writer – that is, having a competitive and insecure job in an industry which, weirdly, doesn't value you very highly – are going to be present whether you like them or not.

There have been entire months, sometimes, when I should have been writing, but have accomplished nothing useful because of some publishing drama which just needed resolution. No one else cares much about such dramas, or at least nothing close to the amount I do, with the result that such things often don't resolve fast.

Your comfort and shelter against those storms? Well, like I say, I don't have any magical answers but, here, for what it's worth, are some things which may help:

Gin. Or cheap wine. Or whatever works. I favour beers from this fine brewery or really cheap Australian plonk. The kind you can thin paints with.

Changing your priorities for a bit. So if you really needed to clear out the garage or redecorate the nursery, then do those things in the time you had thought you'd be writing. You're not losing time; you're just switching things around.

Addressing any emotional/practical issues as fast and practically as you can. So let's say you have book #1 out on submission, you can help yourself by getting the best version of that book out (getting our excellent editorial advice upfront if you need to). You can make sure you go to a minimum of ten agents, and probably more like twelve to fifteen. You can make sure those agents are intelligently chosen, and that your query letter and synopsis are in great shape. (See the PSs for a bit more on this.) You can write yourself a day planner that gives some structure to the waiting process: *X agents queried on 1 May. Eight weeks later is 26 June. At that point, I (a) have an agent, (b) send more queries, (c) get an editor to look at my text, or (d) switch full-steam to the new manuscript*. If you plan things like that upfront, you don't have to waste a bazillion hours crawling over the same questions in your head.

Accepting the reality. It's just nicer accepting when things are blocked or too busy or too fraught. The reality is the same, but the lived experience is nicer. So be kind to yourself.

Find community. Yes, your partner is beautiful and adorable and the joy of your life. But he/she isn't a writer. So he/she doesn't understand you. Join a community. Make friends. Share a moan with people who know exactly what you mean. That matters. It makes a difference.

Enjoy writing. This is the big one, in fact. The writers who most struggle with their vocation are the ones who like having written something, but don't enjoy writing it. And I have to say, I've never understood that. My happiest work times have nearly always been when I'm throwing words down on a page or editing words I've already put there. And that pleasure means you keep on coming back to your manuscript whenever you can. And that means it gets written. And edited. And out to agents or uploaded to KDP and sold.

Of those six, then cultivating that happiness is the single biggest gift you can give yourselves.

And the gin, obviously.

Harry

PS: Want to chat about all this? Then do so on Jericho Townhouse.

PPS: Hate writing? Prefer gin? Then unsubscribe from this email and distil your own. Drink it by the vat.

Fractals, scenes and the bones of the fallen

I've been reading a terrific guest post on our blog by C M Taylor. (And actually, 'guest post' doesn't feel like quite the right term, if I'm honest. Craig's a buddy, not a guest.)

The post is on how to write a scene and, in it, Craig asks:

> *If the theme of your work, say, is unrequited love, does your scene angle in to that theme? Does it demonstrate a circumstance or a feeling which is associated with unrequited love? Or does it demonstrate a circumstance or a feeling about requited love, so as to throw into relief the experience that one of your characters will have about unrequited love?*

And those are interesting questions, aren't they?

I, for one, don't write a book thinking that every scene I write has to 'angle in' to my major theme. But what if that's wrong? What if, in a well-constructed book, pretty much everything angles in to the one same issue? (Or, rather, cluster of issues, because a book that is rich thematically can never be too neatly categorised.)

And here's another thought:

What if you don't especially think about these things as you build your story? What if you do concentrate on good writing (nice prose, strong characters, a well-knitted plot), but don't overthink the thematic stuff?

What happens then? Is the result strong? Or will it never reach the kind of thematic depth and congruence that Craig is hinting at?

Hey, ho. Interesting questions. So I thought I'd take a look at my own work and see what's actually happened there.

So my last book, *The Deepest Grave*, has a cluster of themes that include:

- **Ancient history**, specifically post-Roman Britain and the shade of Arthur.
- **Treasure and fakery.**
- **Death**, because this is a murder mystery, but it is also a book about Fiona Griffiths, whose attitudes to life and death are deep and complicated.

But then, I only have to write those themes down on the page here – something I've never done before; I don't *plan* my thematic stuff – and I realise this: that those themes absolutely and necessarily contain their opposites. So a book that is about fakery and death is also, essentially, a book about:

- **Authenticity.**

- **Life** – or, more specifically in Fiona's case, the whole knotty business of how to be a human; how to establish and maintain an identity in the face of her over-awareness of death.

OK. So those, broadly, are my themes. Let's now look at whether my various scenes tend to hammer away at those things, or not. Are themes something that appear via a few strong, bold story strokes? Or are they there, fractal-like, in every detail too?

And, just to repeat, those aren't questions I consciously think about much as I write. Yes, a bit, sometimes, but I certainly don't go through the disciplined thought process that Craig mentions in his post.

And blow me down, but what I find is that, yes, those themes infest the book. The book never long pulls away from them at all.

So, aside from a place and date stamp at the top of chapter 1, the first words in the book are these:

Jon Breakell has just completed his chef d'oeuvre, his masterpiece. The Mona Lisa of office art. The masterpiece in question is a dinosaur made of bulldog clips, twisted biro innards and a line of erasers that Jon has carved into spikes.

That's a nod towards ancient history. It's a nod towards authenticity (the Mona Lisa) and fakery (a dinosaur that is definitely not a real dinosaur.) It's also, perhaps, a little nod towards death, because in a way the most famous thing about dinosaurs is that they're extinct.

It goes on. The mini-scene that opens the book concludes with Fiona demolishing her friend's dinosaur and the two of them bending down to clear up the mess. Fiona says, *that's how we are—me, Jon, the bones of the fallen—when Dennis Jackson comes in.*

That phrase, *the bones of the fallen*, puts death explicitly on the page and in a way which alludes forward to the whole Arthurian battle theme that will emerge later.

That's one example and – I swear, vow and promise – I didn't plan those links out in my head prior to writing. I just wrote what felt natural for the book that was to come.

But the themes keep on coming. To use Craig's word, all of the most glittering scenes and moments and images in the book keep on angling in to my little collection of themes.

There's a big mid-book art heist and hostage drama. Is there a whiff of something ancient there? Something faked and something real? Of course. The heist is fake and real, both at the same time.

The crime that sits at the heart of the book has fakery at its core. But then Fiona start doubling up on the fakery – she's faking a fake, in effect – but in the process, it turns out, she has created something authentic. And the authenticity of that thing plays a key role in the book's final denouement.

Another example. Fiona's father plays an important role in this book. He's not a complicated or introspective man. He doesn't battle, the way his daughter does, for a sense of identity.

But what happens in the book? This big, modern, uncomplicated man morphs, somehow, into something like a modern Arthur. That identity shift again plays a critical role in the final, decisive dramas. But it echoes around the rest of the book too. Here's one example:

> *Dad drives a silver Range Rover, the car Arthur would have chosen.*
>
> *It hums as it drives, transfiguring the tarmac beneath its wheels into something finer, silvered, noble.*
>
> *A wash of rain. Sunlight on a hill. Our slow-paced Welsh roads.*

That's playful, of course, and I had originally intended just to quote that first line, about the Range Rover. But when I opened up the text, I found the sentences that followed. That one about 'transfiguring the tarmac' is about that process of transformation from something ordinary to something more like treasure, something noble.

And then even the bits that follow that – the wash of rain, the sunlight on the hill – don't those things somehow attach to the *finer, silvered, noble* phrase we've just left? It's as though the *authenticity* of the man driving the Range Rover transforms these ordinary things into something treasured. Something with the whisper of anciency and value.

I could go on, obviously, but this email would turn into a very, very long one if I did.

And look:

Yet again, I've got to the end of a long piece on writing without a real 'how-to' lesson to close it off.

Craig's blog post says, among many other good things, that you should ask whether or not your scene angles in to your themes. But I don't do that. Not consciously, not consistently. And – damn my eyes and boil my boots – I discover that the themes get in there anyway. Yoo-hoo, here we are.

Uninvited, but always welcome.

So the moral of all this is …?

Well, I don't know. I think that, yes, if you're stuck with a scene, or if it's just feeling a little awkward or wrong, then working through Craig's list of scene-checks will sort you out 99% of the time. A conscious, almost mechanical, attention to those things will eliminate problems.

But if you're not the conscious mechanic sort, then having a floaty awareness of the issues touched on in this email will probably work as well. If you maintain that rather unfocused awareness of your themes, you'll find yourself naturally gravitating towards phrases and scenes and metaphors and moments that reliably support the structure you're building.

And that works, I think. The final construction will have both coherence and a kind of unforced naturalness.

And for me, it's one of the biggest pleasures of being an author. That looking back at a text and finding stuff in it that you never consciously put there.

Damn my eyes and boil my boots.
Till soon.

Harry

PS: Want to chat about all this? Then do so on Jericho Townhouse. I'll be there with tea and biscuits. If you're not yet a member, you get an extra biscuit by way of reward.

PPS: One of the questions I'm asked most in those emails is, 'How do I know if now is the right time to get an editorial assessment?'

And my incredibly helpful answer is always – well, I dunno. I'm not you, am I?

But as a rough guide, you want to self-edit as hard as you can and to keep going until you recognise that you're going round in circles, or are totally confused, or if you're just not achieving anything much of real value anymore.

At that point, you have two choices. You can send your stuff out to ten to twelve literary agents, and just see. If your work is strong enough to be marketed, then *boom*! You didn't need that editorial assessment. If agents don't take you on, then you can get the assessment, confident that you do in fact need it. That it's worth the investment.

Alternatively, if you have a sneaky feeling that your work isn't yet agent-ready, then it almost certainly isn't. In which case, a manuscript assessment beckons. It is and has always been the gold-standard way to improve your work. It's always worked for me. It always will.

PPPS: Hate writing? Want to boil your boots for soup? Then unsubscribe from this email and boil away. If I were you, I'd add a bayleaf. Maybe a tad of pepper.

New York gets Daunted

Usually, on Thursday afternoon or so, I start pondering what I'm going to write about on Friday.

This week: no pondering. There's only one thing I could possibly write about.

The biggest book-related newsflash this week – or this year – is that Barnes & Noble is changing ownership. The ins and outs are a little complex (and everything is not quite settled), but if all goes according to plan:

An investment firm, Elliott Advisers, is to buy Barnes & Noble, in a deal which values that business (including its debts) at about $700 million.

That sounds like a lot of money, but given that B&N's sales are $3.6 billion, the pricing actually feels pretty cheap – reflecting the dismal state of B&N.

Elliott is also the 100% owner of Waterstones, the British equivalent of B&N. Both those chains are proper bookshops, appealing to proper book lovers. In that sense, the chains are distinct from the supermarkets, who just sell a lot of books but don't care about them, or the British High Street and travel operator, WHSmith, which is as much a stationer and a newsagent as an actual bookstore.

Waterstones was rescued from impending financial disaster by CEO James Daunt. It was Daunt who negotiated the sale of the firm to Elliott.

Daunt will now act as CEO to both firms – B&N and Waterstones – and will divide his time between London and New York.

As it happens, Daunt also owns and runs his own mini-chain of high-end London bookstores. It was his experience at those stores which won him the position at Waterstones.

So, assuming that all goes according to plan, James Daunt will be the book world's second most powerful human, after Jeff Bezos.

So what does that mean – for readers? For writers? For publishers? For anyone?

Well.

It's a big and important move. James Daunt has a huge reputation in the UK, and it's probably deserved. His secret sauce for success? Quite simply this: there is no secret sauce.

In the UK, Daunt simply took everything back to basics.

He turned bookselling into a proper career. (Albeit, inevitably, a badly paid one.) He retained staff who cared passionately about books and waved goodbye to the rest, perhaps a third of them. He cut costs. He made his stores prettier.

And, in a move so radical that it shook British publishing to its core, *he let each store manager select their own inventory.* So yes, of course, every store was expected to stock major bestsellers of the moment.

But beyond that, what stores sold was guided by local passion and local knowledge. From a reader's point of view, stores got better. There was more energy, more passion, more commitment.

But publishers, for a while, didn't know what to do. In the past, publishing worked like this:

Publishers paid Waterstones a big chunk of cash to get into a 3-for-2 front-of-store promotion. So Waterstones was actually retailing its shelf-space. It wasn't really curating its own retail offering.

Some of those 3-for-2s did really well and became huge bestsellers.

Others didn't, and the volume of returns was enormous (often 20% of total stock).

Publishers pulped those returns, ditched those authors and just made money from their mega-successes.

That was cheque-book publishing and cheque-book retail.

Daunt killed that approach, and terrified publishers. How could they market books if the key step wasn't just throwing bundles of money at retailers?

Well, they solved that problem … kinda. But all they really did was turn their attentions (even more than before) to the supermarkets and other mass retailers. Waterstones' local stores are great and feel like real bookshops … but they can't build a bestseller as they did in the old days, because each store chooses its stock according to its own tastes.

Daunt's path in the US is likely to follow the exact same route. He's commented that one of the issues he feels on entering a typical B&N store is quite simply 'too many books'. Too much stock. Too little curation and guidance. Not enough knowledge from the booksellers. An atmosphere so flat, you could swap it for cigarette paper.

He'll cut stock. Reduce staff, but retain the best and most passionate members. Eliminate central promotions. Get better terms from publishers. Sharply reduce stock returns.

Do the basics, but do them right.

The impacts, positive and negative?

The positive: Elliott's cash plus Daunt's knowhow should save specialist physical book retail in the US. That's massive. It's the difference between a US publishing industry that operates much as it does now and one that would be almost wholly slave to Amazon. That also means that trad publishing is likely to survive in roughly its current shape and size, rather than being sidelined by the growth of digital-first publishers (notably self-pubbers and Amazon itself).

The negative: US publishers will have to learn the lessons already absorbed by the Brits. If B&N no longer operates national promotion systems as in the past, publishers can't make a bestseller just by buying space. Yes, they'll go on seeing what they can do on social media and all that stuff. But, as in the UK, they'll be even more dependent on supermarkets. The make-or-break of a book will be not 'is this wonderful writing?' but 'did we get enough retail space in enough supermarkets at a sufficiently attractive price?'

I know any number of authors where Book A did incredibly well but Book B did poorly ... and Book B was better than Book A. The difference, in every case, was that the supermarkets backed A and not B, and there's damn all a trad publisher can do once the supermarkets have said no.

Oh yes, and supermarkets really don't give a damn about the quality of writing. They don't *know* about the quality of the writing. They buy on the basis of past sales (if you're John Grisham) or a pretty cover (if you're a debut).

Of course, they'd say their selection is a damn sight more careful than that, and it probably is. But that's still 'careful by the standards of people who sell tinned beans for a living'. That's not the same thing as actually being careful.

That sounds like a fairly downbeat conclusion, but the Elliott-saves-B&N news is still a real big plus for anyone who loves traditional stores, print books and traditional publishing. It's the single biggest win I can remember over the past few years.

What that win won't do, however, is weaken the hold of supermarkets and Amazon over book retail. Those two forces are still huge. They're still central.

And of course, talking about print books has its slightly quaint side. Me, I prefer print. I hardly ever read e-books. I spend enough time on screens as it is.

But print books constitute less than 30% of all adult fiction sales, and online print sales accounts for a big chunk of that 30%. In other words, all those B&N stores up and down the US are still only attacking

23% or so of the total adult fiction market. However well Daunt does, that 23% figure isn't about to change radically. (Or not in the direction he wants, anyway.)

But, just for now, to hell with realism. Let's remember the magic of a beautiful bookstore. Daunt does. Here are some comments of his from 2017:

> ... *[there is a sense that] a book bought from a bookshop is a better book ... When a book comes through a letter box or when a book is bought in a supermarket, it's not vested with the authority and the excitement that comes from buying it in a bookshop ... Price is irrelevant if the customer likes the shop. The book is never an expensive item, [particularly for the many customers who] we know are quite happy to go into a café and spend dramatically more on a cup of coffee.*

Quite right, buddy. Now go sell some books. The readers need you.

Till soon.

Harry

PS: Want to chat about all this? Then do so on Jericho Townhouse. I'll be at the door to take your coat and hand you a raspberry macaroon.

PPS: Hey, what about this:

Would you like a literary agent to review and comment on your work?

Would you like to get that feedback from the comfort of your own living room?

Would you like an agent to request your full manuscript, if they like the sample they've reviewed?

For a lot of you, the answer is probably yes. In which case, you'd probably like to know that Jericho members get free access to our regular Slushpile Live webinars – where we stick your work in front of an agent and ask them to comment. We film them as they're commenting and stream the whole thing live. If you have questions, you can just type in your questions and we'll ask the agent on your behalf. And yes, if agents love your stuff, they'll ask for the whole damn manuscript.

All that, as I say, is for Jericho members only – that's the bad news. The good news is: you can take out a JW membership, *for considerably less than the price of a limited edition Lamborghini.*

(And yes, I know, I've got the best sales patter in marketing.)

PPPS: Hate writing? Want to catch up on a lot, a lot, a lot of daytime TV? Then unsubscribe from this stupid email strand right now.

The power of the list

Here are two facts about this ambition/profession of ours that can look daunting:

1. It's damn hard to write a good book.
2. It's damn hard to sell it, once written.

On point 1: well, who cares? If it weren't hard, it wouldn't be fun. You wouldn't have the joy and satisfaction that comes from doing a difficult thing well.

And on 2: well, yes. Good point. Gulp.

It's true that you can write a great book, get a great agent, sell to a great publisher, work hard with a great editor, and then, yes, you stand a chance of selling very well.

It's also possible that you complete those steps, but when the publisher's sales team pitches to the supermarkets, the supermarkets just say no. And if they say no, that's not because you're a terrible author and you've written a terrible book. Those things might be true of course, but the supermarkets wouldn't know. They haven't read your book.

To a huge and underappreciated extent, the race for supermarket sales (as far as debut or near-debut authors is concerned) is like twelve fat men running for the same door. Only one of the runners is going to make it, and which one actually does is a matter of chance more than athleticism.

In short, beyond a point, there's not much you can do to influence sales through bricks-and-mortar retailers. You can go secure that great editor. You can work hard. You can smile sweetly at sales conferences (if you get asked) and all that stuff. But you just can't influence those critical decisions. You aren't even in the room, or anywhere near it.

But all that doesn't mean you can't be highly proactive as a modern author. Nor do you have to self-publish to reap the rewards.

Here's the thing:

The most powerful way to sell on Amazon is via your own mailing list – your very own group of fans.

The detail of building and using that list is relatively intricate. Not because it's so inherently complicated, but because this is an area where detail matters. Exactly how do you solicit email addresses? What do you offer in exchange? What language should you use? How you solve those things can make a huge cumulative difference to how many emails you get (and what quality those emails are).

But that's detail.

The essence of selling via mailing list is really simple:

1. You find people who like your books.

2. You offer them something that they want – probably a shortish story if you're a novelist, something helpful if you're writing subject-led non-fiction.
3. People sign up to get the thing they're after. They also (knowingly and happily) sign up to get regular emails from you.
4. In those emails, you are charming, discursive and helpful … and concentrate fiercely on the topic that brought these readers to you in the first place.
5. When you have a new book to sell, you say, 'Hey guys, do you want my book?'
6. They buy it.

But that's not the clever bit! That's not the bit that explodes your sales and stuffs dollars into your bank account until you fall back, laughing, 'Enough! Enough! Enough!'

The clever bit is this:

7. Amazon notices the sales spike that your emails have generated.
8. Amazon's little marketing robots get so excited that binary starts spouting out of their sockets.
9. Amazon itself starts to pump news of your book out to *all the readers it thinks are most likely to love it*. That'll be via emails, via 'recommended for you' banners, via 'hot new release' promos, and much else.

10. A ton more people start to come across your work … and to buy it … and to discover the wonderful news that you are giving away a wonderful short story …

And the whole process begins again.

This is the critical motor that powers every really successful self-pub author's career. It's the trick that took me to six-figure sales in the US on the back of just six self-published books. It's why even highly advertising-competent authors (like Mark Dawson) say that the three most important things in digital bookselling are 'mailing list, mailing list, mailing list'.

And you can use that trick no matter whether you're planning on a traditional publishing career, or on self-publishing, or on a hybrid of the two. I'd go so far as to say that there are almost no categories of author who shouldn't be thinking of building and nurturing an email list.

Say, for example, you are traditionally published, but your publisher just messes up. You have the advance, but your book sales are disappointing, and your career looks fatally wounded. If you emerge from the wreckage with the start of a decent mailing list, then you have built an asset that will support and protect you for years and years to come. My US trad-publishing career *did* crash and burn (thanks, Random House!), but my US publishing career just went from strength to strength.

Good books + mailing list = a strategy that never fails.

And two other plus points:

A mailing list prompts you to write a 'reader magnet'. That magnet doesn't have to be – and shouldn't be – a full-length book. I use two magnets for my fiction: one of 7,000 words, one of 13,000. Those things are too long for short stories. They're way too short for any publisher to want to buy and print them.

But they're fun to write! And great for readers! They feel like a holiday from work, while being absolutely core to the work you want to do.

And hey: once you have a mailing list, *you can do almost anything*. If you're minded to write a 25,000 word story – for which, to repeat, no traditional publisher would pay – then you can write it and sell it via your mailing list, for $0.99 if you're feeling generous, or $2.99 if you're not. The basic mailing list strategy will still (once your list is somewhat mature) deliver real dividends.

If I had to pick just one brilliant thing about publishing in the last decade or so, I'd have to pick the rise of Amazon and the e-book. If I got to pick two, I'd pick the list-driven sales strategy every time. Nothing, but nothing, but nothing, has empowered authors more.

That's true if you're trad.

It's true if you're indie.

It's true if you're an exciting hybrid of the two, with the head of a goat on the body of a donkey.

That's it from me. It's sunny. And in the cricket, England are about to start batting ...

Till soon.

Harry

PS: Want to chat about all this? Then do so on Jericho Townhouse. I'll be at the door with a glass of prosecco and a dish of strawberries.

PPS: Hate writing? Want to watch cricket until your eyes pop? Course you do. Start by unsubscribing from this silly, silly email.

How to title a book

Of all the writing habits I have, one of the worst – the worst from a good financial sense point of view – is that I like writing LONG books.

My first novel was a spine-breaking 180,000 words. Not one of my novels has ever been less than 110,000 words. The first 'short story' I wrote was 8,000 words, which is to say miles too long to be an actual short story. Heck, even this email is likely to be far longer than any other email you get in your inbox today.

Ah well. There are some things you can't fight, and my addiction to length is one of them.

But that also means that when it comes to short-form copy, I'm at a loss.

I'm not especially good at book blurbs, which want to be about 100–120 words (depending a bit on layouts and where you're expecting them to appear). Since titles need to be short and punchy, I'm not especially good at those either.

In a word: I'm pretty damn rubbish when it comes to coming up with titles … and this email is going to tell you how to write them.

Which means if you want to ignore the entire contents of what follows, on the basis that I obviously, obviously, obviously don't know what I'm talking about, then the evidence is very much in your favour.

That said, I think it's clear enough what a title needs to do. It wants to:

- Be highly consistent with your **genre**.
- **Offer some intrigue** – for example, launch a question in the mind of the reader.
- Ideally, encapsulate '**the promise of the premise**' in a few very short words, distilling the essence of your idea down to its very purest form.

Consistency with genre is the most essential (and the easiest) of these to achieve. It matters a lot now that so many books are being bought on Amazon, because book covers – at the title selection stage – are no more than thumbnails. A bit bigger than a phone icon, but really not much. So yes, the cover has to work hard and successfully in thumbnail form, but the title has more work to do now than it did before.

Genre consistency is therefore key. Your title has to say to your target readers, 'this is the sort of book that readers like you like.' It has to invite the click through to your book page itself. That's its task.

The intrigue is harder to do, but also kinda obvious. *Gone Girl* works because of the 'go girl/gone girl' pun, and those double Gs, and the brevity. But it also works because it launches a question in the mind of the reader: Who is this girl and why has she gone? By contrast, *The Girl on the Train* feels a little flat to me. There are lots of women on lots of trains. There's nothing particularly evocative or intriguing in the image. I don't, as it happens, think that the book was much good, but I don't think the title stood out either. (I think the book sold well because of some pale resemblances between the excellent *Gone Girl* and its lacklustre sister. The trade, desperate for a follow-up hit to *Gone Girl*, pounced on whatever it had.)

The third element in a successful title – the 'promise of the premise' one – is really hard to do. I've not often managed it, and I've probably had a slightly less successful career as a result.

So what works? Well, here are some examples of titles that do absolutely nail it:

The Girl with the Dragon Tattoo
Brilliant! That title didn't translate the rather dour and serious Swedish original, *Man Som Hatar Kvinnor* (*Men Who Hate Women*). Rather, it took the brilliance of the central character and captured her in six words. She was a girl (vulnerable), and she had a tattoo (tough and subversive), and the tattoo was of a dragon (exotic and dangerous). That mixture of terms put the promise of the book's premise right onto the front cover and propelled the book's explosive success.

Incidentally, you'll notice that the title also completely excludes mention of Mikael Blomkvist, who is as central to that first book as Salander is. But no one bought the book for Blomkvist and no one remembers the book for Blomkvist either. So the title cut him out, and did the right thing in doing so.

The Da Vinci Code

Brilliant. Dan Brown is fairly limited as a writer, but it was a stroke of genius to glue together the idea of ancient cultural artefacts with some kind of secret code. Stir those two things up with a bit of Holy Grail myth-making, and the result (for his audience) was commercial dynamite.

And – boom! – that dynamite was right there in the title too. The 'Da Vinci' part namechecks the world's most famous artist. The 'Code' part promises that there are secret codes to be unravelled.

Four words delivering the promise of the premise in full.

I Let You Go

This was Clare Mackintosh's breakout hit, about a mother whose young son was killed in a hit-and-run car accident. The promise of the premise is right there in four very short words … and is given a first-person twist, which just adds a extra bite to the hook in question. A brilliant bit of title-making.

So that's what a title wants to do. A few last comments to finish off.

One, it's quite rare that a title alone does much to propel sales success.

Because there are a lot of books out there, and because everyone's trying to do the same thing, there's not much chance to be genuinely distinctive. My fifth Fiona Griffiths novel was called *The Dead House*, but there are at least three other books on Amazon with that title, or something very like it. That didn't make my title bad, in fact – it did the 'promise of the premise' thing just fine – but I certainly couldn't say my title was so distinctive it did anything much for sales.

Two, if you're going for trad publishing, it's worth remembering that absolutely any title you have in mind at the moment is effectively provisional. If your publishers don't like it, they'll ask you to change it. And if they don't like your title #2, they'll ask you to come up with some others. In short, if, like me, you're bad at titles, you just don't need to worry too much (if you're going the trad-publishing route, that is). There'll be plenty of opportunity to hone your choice well prior to publication.

Three, you don't want to think about title in isolation. There should, ideally, be a kind of reverberation between your title and the cover. That reverberation should be oblique rather than direct. Clare Mackintosh's *I Let You Go* had for its cover image a butterfly trapped against a window – a metaphorical reference to the anguish of the book's premise. If instead it had shown a mother obviously distraught as a car struck her son, the cover – and title – would have seemed painfully clunky and ridiculous.

If you get a great cover image that doesn't work with your chosen title, then change the title. If you have a superb title and your cover designer's image is too directly an illustration of it, then change the image. That title/cover pairing is crucial to your sales success, so you can afford no half-measures in getting it right.

That's all from me.

My kids are making elderflower cordial and singing as they do so. They are also wearing helmets for no reason that I can possibly understand.

Till soon.

Harry

PS: Want to know what I think of your title? Then I'll tell you. Just come over to Jericho Townhouse and pop your title (plus a short description of your book) in the comments. I'll tell you what I think.

PPS: Hate writing? Want to wear helmets while safely indoors and for absolutely no reason at all? Feel free to do so, but you'll want to unsubscribe first.

Why bad reviews make me happy

On 4 August 2017, I got this terrific review from a reader named Anne Hill in the US:

THE MOST BORING BOOK EVER WRITTEN
I'm afraid this is the most boring book I have ever struggled through. Boring beyond belief. It really does not deserve any stars at all in my opinion. Although spelling and grammar were all they should be, the heroine is a most unbelievable and implausible individual ever created. What woman of 5ft 2 inches can be attacked simultaneously by four baddies and either kill or maim them without a scratch to herself. Through the book there were people mentioned without explanation as to who they were. So it did not feel as if one was reading the first book at all. Most confusing. The entire book did just not gel at all.

That was savage, but it wasn't nearly as concise as this one from Mary Claude:

ONE STAR
Didn't read.

What I really want to know about that review, Mary, was whether you read any of it at all? I mean, was the one star an expression of bitter regret that you'd spent $0.99 on an e-book that wasn't really your thing? Or did you read the first page and then just think, Aargh, this is terrible? I don't know, but I love your economy of expression.

My absolute all-time favourite bad review, however, said this (thanks, Assegai):

FIONA GRIFFITHS LEAVES ME QUEASY
Sorry, but when the heroine of the book starts feeling around inside the skull of an autopsied murder victim it really doesn't leave me feeling warm and fuzzy or wanting to read more or learn what makes her tick ... I can deal with quirky, but Fiona Griffiths is FAR beyond quirky and well into mentally ill! I skimmed through the chapters after the night in the morgue just to see how the author resolved things. The answer is not in a particularly believable fashion. Glad I didn't take the word of the critics and buy more than one book in the series. I found Hannibal Lecter a more understandable and sympathetic character.

And look, one of the reasons why I genuinely don't care about these terrible reviews is that they're in a tiny minority. My first Fiona Griffiths book has an average 4.4 rating on Amazon. The latest one hits 4.8 stars. Overall, I have hundreds, even thousands, of 4- and 5-star reviews. So I'm in the nice position of not really having to care about a few negative comments.

But bad reviews do something else as well. They start to segregate your audience, and that's great.

Because here's the thing. In the bad old days, marketing was quite untargeted. My first book came out in February 2000, and it got huge posters on the London Underground and mainline rail stations, probably a few airports too. They even – this is real – had women in blue sashes handing out little three-chapter samplers of the book to passing commuters.

All this was thrilling to see for a newbie author … but the targeting behind that campaign was crazily broad. Based on the reach of some of those posters, my publisher saw my audience as: 'All British commuters using mainline railway stations into London.' And sure, there was an overlap between people-who-use-trains and people-who-like-my-books, but there's no marketing magic there. It's blunderbus, not sniper's rifle. And that wasn't surprising. Back then, there was no alternative.

The internet has changed all that, of course. The trick of marketing anything online these days is to find your audience in the most granular way you possibly can.

That's how come advertising on Facebook works so well. You don't have to market to people-who-use-trains. You can market to people-who-read-and-enjoy-books-like-mine.

That's why email marketing works so well, because you have a direct connection to people who have positively invited your efforts to keep in touch.

That's how come Amazon itself works so well. Go to Amazon's home page and look at the 'recommended for you' bit at the top. Now look at your sister's version of the same page. Or your dad's. Or your children's. Or your friends'. Assuming they're logged into their Amazon account, those pages will always be personalised according to what Amazon knows about your buying habits.

And that's why negative reviews can actually be helpful.

Anyone who's squeamish about my main character and the way she talks and the things she gets up to is never going to be a great reader of my books. Yes, they might buy one book on the off-chance, but then never again. If that person leaves a review because they didn't like X, then readers who are similar will move away and select a more appropriate title for them. That's a win! Increasingly, Amazon won't just know who might buy a single book by Harry Bingham. It'll know who's likely to invest in the whole series. And because selling a whole series is more profitable than just a single book, Amazon will have ever greater confidence in marketing hard to the exact right readership.

It's even the same thing with the reviewer who just said that my book was boring. That review stood alongside a zillion reviews that said it was great. So readers have to think: is this book boring or great?

And, I think if you peruse the reviews in depth, an intelligent reader will figure out that my books don't do a lot of gunfights and car chases but do offer complex and absorbing plots led by a very complex and (I hope) absorbing character.

So the gun-fight-'n'-car-chase readership will go elsewhere. My readership will flock to me.

And again, that's a win. I'd much, much rather a passionate following from a narrow segment of the reading population, than a 'yeah, it's OK' reaction from a large segment.

I'll say more about this kind of thing in future emails: why granularity matters so much and how to exploit it for your benefit.

For now, though, just keep in mind the headline. Granularity matters. Passion matters. A passionate and narrow readership is worth ten times a broad but unpassionate one.

And that headline should guide everything you do, including how you write your books. So if you write a scene and think, 'Aunt Marge likes crime fiction, but she wouldn't like this scene, so I'd better tone it down,' you are thinking the exact wrong thing. You should think, 'Aunt Marge would hate this, but my ideal reader would love it. I wonder if I can find a way to ramp things up even further.'

That strategy will work for you every single time. And it's much, much more fun.

Sorry, Aunt Marge.

Harry

PS: Got some terrible reviews you want to share? Want to talk more about this email? Join me over at Jericho Townhouse. Crumpets available. Aunt Marge not invited.

If you want to talk to me about anything else, then don't be shy. I'm human, the reply button is there for a reason, and I don't bite.

PPS: Hate writing? You actually are Aunt Marge and you're very angry about this email? Well, sorry, Marge. Unsubscribe, and be done with this foolishness.

Stick or twist?

I'm going to talk today about one of the toughest decisions in any author's career.

A few years back, the keynote speaker at our annual Festival of Writing was the brilliant Antonia Hodgson, author of the massively acclaimed, hugely bestselling debut, *The Devil in the Marshalsea*.

Because Antonia was also editorial director at Little, Brown, it seemed a little bit like this was just how publishing happened, if you were part of the in-crowd. You have all these amazing connections. You hone your self-editing skills by editing professionally for many years. You have a glorious outcome.

That's a nice story, in a way, except it didn't really feel like it was very relevant to an audience of aspiring writers, not one of whom happened to be the editorial director of an internationally respected publisher.

Only here's the thing –

The Devil in the Marshalsea wasn't Antonia's first book. It was her first *published* book.

Her first manuscript was a 250,000-word vampire novel written long after the whole vampire wave had risen and crashed.

It was, from the sound of it, a terrible book. And, for all her mighty editorial prowess, it took a literary agent to sit Antonia down and tell her the bad news.

So what do we make of that? What do we learn?

Well, we learn that Antonia Hodgson is like us after all. And that she had the guts to ditch one monster manuscript and start all over again.

But also: writing a first novel is hard. It may not work. It may not work, even if you put your intelligent damnedest into fixing up that first draft.

Indeed, we see this all the time with our editorial clients. Yes, some of them make a brilliant go of their first novel. But for others, the first novel is basically a learning experience. A sandbox where you can make every mistake in the book and then learn to fix it.

But you can make 100 mistakes and fix every one, and sometimes what you're left with is a good novel. A technically proficient, interesting, decently written, good novel.

And (sorry!) that's not enough. The top few percent of every agent's slush pile will consist of good, competent novels. No one ever woke up in the morning and thought, 'Must head to Amazon and see if they have any good, competent novels in stock.'

The fact is that we – readers, agents, editors – want to be dazzled and transported. We want to be blown away. And a novel that gets laboriously worked and re-worked just may not retain that dazzle.

Indeed, it's more than likely that the original concept was flawed. It's quite likely that the writer didn't really go for it when designing the basic story set-up. That they played safe rather than going all in. (Or, another error: they went all-in on a story that no audience actually wants.)

And look: writing is hard.

Nothing here is saying, 'You've done this wrong. You're a terrible human. Go and learn golf, because you don't belong on our planet.'

Quite the opposite. I'm saying that for many writers – not all, but most – there'll come a point where you think, 'This story isn't working, and I can't fix it.'

And that's OK. You're learning. Sometimes a dodgy first novel is part of the learning. Fine. Don't stress.

I do think it's a good idea to self-edit the thing hard. There are two reasons for that. First, you learn by editing. Second, most great novels look pretty dire in those early drafts. You don't quite know what you're dealing with until you've done some editing work.

But let's say you've self-edited hard. Perhaps you've worked with us editorially. Perhaps you've taken a course or come to the Festival of Writing.

You've done all that good stuff and … the book still isn't working.

Good.

You've achieved your most important task, which was to learn a hell of a lot about writing. The best way to write a good book is often enough to write a bad one first. That's not failure. That's apprenticeship.

And you know what? Writing a first novel that goes on to become a bestseller isn't necessarily the gift you might think it is.

My first novel *did* get picked up by agents, *did* get fought over at auction and *did* become a bestseller. So I thought, ha! I know how to write books.

But I didn't, because I'd had a curtailed, weird apprenticeship. My second book was a total disaster. So bad, I deleted it and started again. That's hard enough at any time, but I was mid-contract with HarperCollins and the whole episode felt seriously alarming. I rescued things, but the experience was no fun at all.

One last thing.

A lot of you will want to ask: *how do I know?* How can I tell when it's time to move on?

Well, I don't know. Sorry.

What I will say is that the experience of moving on can be both scary and liberating. Scary, because you have to release something you've been highly attached to. Liberating, because once you let go of that attachment, your imagination surges with all the other great things you could be writing about.

Antonia Hodgson started with vampires. She made her name with historical crime fiction. Who knows what could lie in store for you?

Till soon.

Harry

PS: Want to chat about this email? Let's meet in Townhouse and do just that.

PPS: Hate writing? Prefer to read a competently written novel or two? Then unsubscribe. We'll miss you, though.

The probable and the plausible

I watched a film on TV the other night. The film was Denis Villeneuve's *Sicario*, a thriller dealing with the drugs trade on both sides of the US-Mexican border. The film was released in 2015 but drew its inspiration from a period a few years earlier, when drugs-related violence was at its height.

And –

The film is essentially a lie. It treats the Mexican city of Ciudad Juarez much as you might deal with Baghdad or Kabul: a territory where every street corner threatens to conceal a sniper or an IED.

The film also implies that the American war on drugs has become almost entirely extra-legal. That there is no longer any meaningful attempt to arrest, prosecute and convict drug barons. It implies also that the state-level US police in those border territories are so riven with corruption that you can't trust any of them.

None of this is really true. Yes, Mexico has had a serious problem with gang violence. At the same time, Juarez is a major industrial city that does massive legitimate trade with the US. And Mexico, unlike Iraq or Afghanistan, is the kind of place that a reasonable person might choose to visit for vacation. And if I lost my wallet in Tucson, I'd hardly be worried about asking a police officer for help.

In short, the film has its roots in facts, but it has its trunk, leaves and branches where they should be. On Planet Fiction. The world of make-believe.

It's a combination I know well myself. My last full-length book was a modern-day police procedural about the quest for Arthur. Arthur as in King Arthur, a man whose very existence is uncertain.

Yes, I took care to make sure that my lower-level facts were all true. I took care with things like my description of hillforts, ancient manuscript references to Arthur, some science on the dating – and faking – of artefacts, and so on. But I only took care with these things because I wanted to use them as a springboard into the delights of sheer invention.

When I published that book, I was a little worried about the reaction of my audience. My readers are crime readers, and that genre, above all, is a realistic one.

But –

They didn't care. No one did. My reader reviews for that book averaged a full 5.0 on Amazon.com for a long time and have since dipped to 4.8. No book of mine has done better.

The simple fact is that you *do* need to write fiction that feels plausible. You *do not* need to write fiction that feels remotely probable, or even possible.

How do you achieve that plausibility? Well, the full answer would probably be a rather long one, so let me offer these three thoughts:

Thought the first

Deploy those 'lower-level' facts, as I've called them, as diligently as you can. Where your fiction touches ordinary life, make sure that you are as precise as you can be. In my case, I didn't just invent a South Welsh hillfort. I searched around until I found one that fit the bill. Then I got in a car and visited it. The facts that I reported in the book – about evidence of jewellery-making, a large number of animal bones, and so on – are all spot on.

It's not even that readers will know whether your facts are right or not. It's that those facts will give your imagination enough security to leap without fear. The gap between truth and fiction will be invisible to the reader.

Thought the second

I keep coming back to this, and it surprises me. But honestly, I think great descriptive writing has a huge role to play here. A rootedness in place will give everything else you write a kind of plausibility.

In *Sicario*, there are quite long bits of film that are just shots of landscape. That sounds dull, in a way, but add some moody music and a tense story situation, and those shots just deepen your involvement in everything else. But also, they act as a kind of guarantor of reality. 'Look, these are real places. There's nothing tricksy or staged about this filming. The story must be real, because these places clearly are.'

That's nonsense logic, of course, but humans aren't especially logical. And by the way, this approach works no matter what kind of book you're writing.

In my case (and that of *Sicario*), those places are real. They're contemporary. You can go and visit them. But the same basic point applies to any book, whether you're dealing with the court of Catherine the Great, or some planet in a far-flung galaxy. If you can get the reader, as it were, feeling the wind on their face and the sand between their toes, you are at least halfway to convincing them of everything else.

Thought the third
This is the big one. The ultimate plausibility trick.

In *Sicario*, the central character is Kate Macer, an FBI agent played by Emily Blunt. And she doesn't really *do* anything. You could take her out of the film and the plot could (just about) unroll the same way. Her role is that of observer and interpreter. She witnesses the same things as we witness, but by interpreting those things through her own (pained, horrified) emotions, she explains to us what we should be feeling too.

Now, I don't really recommend turning your protagonist into an observer only. That's not an impossible technique (the Sherlock Holmes stories are narrated by Dr Watson, after all), but it's a tricky one. On the other hand, films are films and books are books, and that's a bone we don't need to worry at now.

The point is simply this:

In *Sicario*, we see and believe in Kate Macer's emotional journey. And she wouldn't react that way if she wasn't seeing real things. Ergo, the story she witnesses must be real. *Boom!* Case closed. Job done. Game, set and match.

The way to get your stories feeling plausible, no matter how implausible they actually are, is to plant a real-feeling character in a real-feeling landscape, then watch like a hawk as his or her emotions unfold.

That's all from me for now. I'm off to enjoy the English summer (brolly in hand).

Till soon.

Harry

PS: Want to chat about this email? Get your brolly out and we'll meet over at Jericho Townhouse. If you're not yet a member of Townhouse, then tush and pish.

PPS: Hate writing? Whizzing off to Baghdad/Kabul/Damascus for holiday? Then unsubscribe first. You'll be glad you did.

The internal and the external

You all know about outer jeopardy and inner conflict, right? So if you have a protagonist with some great fear of spiders, you sort of know the climactic scenes are going to involve a spider farm, or a genetically modified giant spider, or something of that sort.

To take a slightly more grown-up example, the climax of *Pride and Prejudice* deals in the same themes that have seeded the entire book (love and marriage; maturity and immaturity; sober judgement and impulsive decisions). The inner stuff and the outer stuff all run in parallel.

And that's all good. That's all part of good writing.

But there's a more interesting way to join inner and outer. It won't work for every book, or not in its more dramatic manifestations. But it's still interesting enough that I want to put the thought in front of you anyway.

Here's how it works.

You identify a deep conflict you want to explore.

Ideally, that conflict should exist at a personal level, as well as a bigger, social, level. So you might think about power struggles between a man and a woman within a marriage, but you might also think about those things more broadly within society. We're still talking about an essentially inner conflict, however.

Then, you externalise that conflict, but on a massive scale. You don't just write a portrait of a marriage, for example, you imagine a future where women are owned for their reproductive capacity. Boom: you've got Margaret Atwood's *The Handmaid's Tale*.

Or you imagine a world where humans are hermaphrodite and just have seasonal biological changes that flip them into (temporary) men or (temporary) women. And boom: you've got Ursula K. Le Guin's classic novel, *The Left Hand of Darkness*.

Another example.

You know that thing you get in a large city – London or New York, let's say – where rich and poor inhabit the same physical city, yet live completely separate lives. Or you could think about a city like Belfast, where separation is effected via religion, not wealth or race etc.

And, yes, you could write an interesting, carefully observed, realist novel about those things – or you could do what China Miéville did in *The City & the City*, and just create a world where the people of one world almost literally couldn't 'see' the people of the other, and vice versa.

In all these cases – Miéville, Le Guin, Atwood – the power of their stories came from the way they took an interesting personal/psychological/social issue and externalised it on a massive scale – citywide, countrywide, planetary.

Now, it's not surprising that the examples I've drawn are from speculative fiction. This particular trick is quite close to defining what speculative fiction actually is. It's the thing that lies right at the core of the art form.

But ... you don't have to write speculative fiction to use the same basic ploy.

Take, for example, the Cold War novels of John le Carré.

Le Carré wanted to write about love and betrayal, and in particular the idea that all human loving relationships would end up in betrayal. (That's a very bleak view and not actually true to life. But you can write great fiction while not being true to life.)

Now, again, he could just have written a stony, cold love story, in which everyone betrays everyone. But what would have been the resonance of that? Not a lot, one would guess.

His flash of genius was to set that basic story in the world of Cold War espionage, where everyone really did betray everyone, and where nuclear weapons were pointing at major world capitals, and things (from a certain plausible perspective) really did seem unutterably bleak.

And boom: that combination of inner and outer conflicts mirroring each other produced some of the greatest novels of post-war British fiction: *The Spy Who Came In from the Cold* and *Tinker, Tailor, Soldier, Spy*, together with the others in that sequence.

To jump from some of the greatest ever works of literature to, ahem, my own work: I do the same thing. I don't do it on the Atwood/Le Guin scale, by any means, but:

Internal conflict: My character is in recovery from Cotard's Syndrome, a genuine condition in which sufferers believe themselves to be dead. My character is constantly grappling with what it is to be alive.

External conflict: And my character's job is that of … homicide detective. So her day job constantly brings her up against the same things that trouble her in her personal life.

That unity of inner and outer just adds force to every element of the tale. The murder stories have a bigger resonance. The personal-angst stuff feels integral not gratuitous.

In other words, even if you don't choose to go all-out Atwood-Le Guin-Miéville, you can still borrow the same basic technique. It's a brilliant tool, and I love it, and now you should go and play with it yourself.

Don't hurt yourself though. Tools can be sharp.

Till soon.

Harry

PS: Tell me about your manuscript. Do you have an inner/outer symmetry that parallels some of the examples I've given above? Come over to Jericho Townhouse and tell me.

PPS: Just to be quite clear, membership of Jericho Writers does not give you a free car.

It doesn't make you younger, better-looking, or more popular.

Contrary to widespread rumour, JW membership will **not** give you total, dictatorial control over a small but prosperous country.

On the other hand, a JW membership does help you write better, publish better and give you an infinitude of creative satisfaction. Forget that small but prosperous country, and do what you gotta do. Your manuscript will bob a curtsey and say a very courteous thank you.

PPPS: Hate writing? Handmaid causing trouble again? Do what you need to do and unsubscribe. Damn those handmaids. They're always awkward.

I love deadlines

I love deadlines. You know why? Because I love that whooshing sound they make as they go by. (That's a Douglas Adams joke, if you didn't already know.)

And that's the subject of today's email, because – I completely forgot it was Friday and I haven't written one solitary word. If you were looking for loving, wise counsel on all matters writer – well, sorry, buddy, I ain't got nothing for ya.

Sorry.

That's it from me. I'll do better next week – I do most solemnly swear thereto. Oh yes, and to make up: if you have a question to ask me, then just hit reply. I always say that, I know, but this time I'm saying it extra. Hit reply. Tell me what's on your mind, on all matters writerly.

Till soon.

Harry

How to market yourself and your book – in two words

Today I'm going to talk about marketing. That's a conundrum for:

- **Self-published authors**, because if they don't market their work, then no one else will.
- **Traditionally published authors**, because an increasing amount of the marketing load will fall on them, no matter what.
- **Not-yet-published authors**, because you guys still have to market yourself to agents or whoever else in due course.

And although authors are a pretty diverse bunch, they're generally united in really, really, really hating the whole business of self-promotion. The brash, self-loving types who make confident hucksters have an approximately 0% overlap with the sort of people who scurry off to a quiet place to write down the pictures they have in their head.

And good news:

That brash hucksterism just doesn't work in the world of books. You don't have to do it. If you do, you'll fail.

And more good news:

Doing marketing right is easy. I'll tell you in just two words what it's all about. (Though obviously this email will be the normal thousand-word whopper, because I don't do short.)

The first word that needs to discipline everything you ever do on the marketing front is simply: *authenticity*.

If you're not authentic in your marketing, it'll never succeed. So let's say you're coming to the Festival of Writing this September. Obviously, you'll want to meet and talk to some agents. (The same goes for any similar writers' conference, of course.)

So be yourself.

Nothing else will be remotely convincing to the agent. If you try to fake some hyper-extrovert brashness, you'll come over as a clown or a fool. (Unless you are hyper-extrovert, in which case, fine. Be yourself.) Agents would far, far rather meet a writer who speaks with sincerity and truthfulness than someone who tries to sell in a pushy way.

Same thing for trad-published authors. If you hate and loathe Twitter, for example, you'll be crap at it. You can't goad yourself into being something you're not. So just tell your publishing team that you hate Twitter, and they'll structure their marketing campaigns to take that into account.

Same thing for self-published authors. Readers sign up to your mailing list because they want to hear from you, not from some weird, constructed alter-ego. You may notice that these emails from me sound authentically me – because they are! I say what I think, and I express myself the way I like expressing myself. The real me and the email me are one and the same. (Except that the real me is devilishly handsome, of course.)

Which brings us to the second massive requirement on your marketing efforts: *strategy*.

You need to be authentic, but always strategic. Those two things together (plus time) are a lethally powerful combination.

So again:

If you're going to a writers' conference, wanting to meet and talk to agents, then research them beforehand. Who's coming? Who looks like a great fit for you? Make little cheat sheets for who you'd like to meet and include key data about why you like them. Include little printed photos, so you can be sure you recognise them when you see them across a dining hall. Remind yourself of what you want to ask before getting into that conversation. And if you are in the midst of a long but inessential conversation with a fellow writer as Your Perfect Agent queues to get coffee, then break off that long but inessential conversation. (Politely, of course, because the authentic you is always polite.)

Same thing with trad authors. If, for example, you're invited to a meet-the-trade evening, figure out who's going to be there. Figure out who you want to talk to. Make damn sure you spend as much time hearing from the other person about what they do as you spend talking about yourself. And if you are on Twitter, then cultivate followers and influencers who are relevant to you. Be authentic and strategic.

Self-pub: the same thing, but squared. There's an inconceivably huge number of ways to market your work. You're going to be authentic in everything you do. Your ads will truthfully reflect your work. Your emails will sound like you. Your Facebook content will vibrate with personality and genuineness.

But you'll prioritise. Which sales channels work? What's just fluff? When do you kill a series? How much time do you spend replying to reader comments and questions?

I can't in fact think of a single author/book marketing issue, broadly defined, where the *authentic + strategic* combination isn't the right one to adopt. Make those two commandments central to everything you do, and you'll be fine.

Till soon.

Harry

PS: Got a marketing conundrum? And yes, I'm including the conundrum of not-yet-published authors trying to break into the trad-publishing world. If you've got any kind of self-marketing conundrum, just come over to Jericho Townhouse and tell me.

PPS: Yes, I know. The 'be strategic' commandment looks smart, but it does beg the question of what the right strategy is. That's as true of trad publishing as it is of self-pub. Both things are hard, and you simply have to be strategically competent to excel. So how do you know? How do you navigate those minefields as a newbie, when pretty much everyone who matters knows more than you do? Well, you probably want to get your nose into the most comprehensive set of tools and courses available anywhere – tools and courses that are free to members of Jericho Writers. If you sign up today, we will gift-wrap a small brown calf and send it to you, with our compliments.

PPPS: That thing about gift-wrapping a calf: it's not true. Sorry.

PPPPS: Hate writing? Want to navigate some real minefields? Then unsubscribe. We're not for you.

So wrong, it's right

The first time one of my Fiona Griffiths novels went to a copyeditor, no one had thought to check with me what I actually wanted from the process. (Which, ahem, is not absolutely unheard of in trad publishing.)

My FG novels are voiced by my heroine herself. She sounds like this:

> *We find signs to Porthgain, the village, but a small white sign points us further up the coast. 'Porthgain Secure Hospital'.*
>
> *A one-way track, unhedged.*
> *A pale sea rising on the horizon.*
>
> *We drive for a mile or two. Then, at a turn in the road, a gleam of white buildings occupying their own narrow headland. A jut of rock.*

Now, as you may notice, Fiona Griffiths doesn't write the way you were taught to write at school. She uses sentence fragments, a lot. (A sentence fragment lacks a main verb, as for example, 'A one-way track, unhedged.') She uses some extremely short paragraphs, including plenty of one-worders. She never uses a semi-colon. She'll often make a list where items are separated by full stops (Brit-speak for 'periods') instead of commas and so on.

In short, she offends the instinct of every good copyeditor everywhere in the world.

Now, it turned out that my friends at Orion had, in their goodness, decided to unfreeze a cryogenically preserved librarian from the 1950s. They'd thawed off the tweed, recurled the hair, and had her spectacles specially reframed to be extra scary. They then asked this fine lady to copyedit the work of Detective Sergeant Fiona Griffiths.

And –

The result was not a happy one. Sentence fragments got resentenced. Those lists-with-full-stops got remade into regular comma-style lists. Semi-colons entered the manuscript in their swarms.

My nice clean prose turned from stuff like this:

A one-way track, unhedged.
 A pale sea rising on the horizon.
 We drive for a mile or two. [...]

To stuff like this:

The track is one way and unhedged. On the horizon, a pale sea rises up and we drive on for a mile or two. [...]

And, you know, that kind of writing is really fine. Most people write with plenty of main verbs. I use 'em myself. I've got nothing against them.

But –

That's not how Fiona Griffiths writes or sounds or is. So when I got the completed revised manuscript back again, I just said no.

No, that wasn't how I wanted it. No, that wasn't the voice of Fiona Griffiths that I'd so carefully contrived. And, in short, just no, no, no. (There was a swearier version too, but I kept that to myself.)

So Orion, bless 'em, said, 'You're quite right. We were wrong. We'll put it all back.' And they did, except that they cleaned up any actual typos and the rest.

So good. That sounds like a win for common sense and late-blooming editorial tact.

But what I want to say is this:

There are no rules that matter except those of clarity and expressive force. If you are clear and expressive, your writing is just fine, and phooey to anyone who says different.

It's fine to repeat yourself. There's T.S. Eliot's much-quoted repetition about 'Time past and time present are both perhaps present in time future' and yes, that's repetitive, but it's also poetry, so maybe doesn't count.

Except you don't need to be one of the greatest poets of all time to get away with a spot of repetition. Here, in a rather humbler context, is Fiona Griffiths doing the exact same thing:

Is Jared Coad the man we snapped in that kebab shop?

I don't know. Just going on the facial resemblance alone, I'd have to say definitely possible. Throw in Coad's combat training and psychological profile, and you'd have to say definitely yes. But throw in the 'oh, but he's in a supermax secure psychiatric facility,' and you're left with – I don't know. The definite yes and the definite no both seem emphatic.

That's four versions of 'definite' in one short paragraph. But is the repetition annoying? I don't think so. To my ear, that paragraph sounds fine and I'd happily defend it from any tweedy librarian.

You may note as well that that paragraph has plenty of contractions ('I'd' for 'I would', for example), which you're not really meant to do. It also makes a noun of the entire phrase 'oh, but he's in a supermax secure psychiatric facility', which is so wrong I don't even know the name for what kind of wrong it is.

But so what?

Clarity, right? And expressive force. That paragraph has both.

You can even (sometimes, not often) make good use of outright clumsiness. In one of the books, Fiona's dad gives her mother a giant silver trophy for the 'World's Best Mam'. It's awful and her mother hates it, but her father, undeterred, fixes it over the kitchen door. Fiona says, 'On the way through into the kitchen, we had to stop to admire the trophy, which now looms over the kitchen door like something about to collapse.'

And that last phrase 'like something about to collapse' doesn't offend against old-fashioned grammar exactly, but it does break good writing guidelines on specificity and elegance. 'Like a tumbledown shed' is what you're meant to say. Or 'like a motorway carwreck'. Or something you can actually put a picture to.

Except that – the phrase itself is clumsy and somehow jury-rigged. Like the shelf which holds the trophy, the actual description feels like a thing on the point of collapse. In other words, I doubt if I could find a better phrase, no matter how long I thought about it.

So in short, in short, in short –

Do what you want.

Yes, you need to develop a good and sensitive ear and a keen sense of the kind of prose you want to hear yourself writing. But do all those good things, then write however the hell you want. Clarity and expressive force. Those two things, forever and always. You don't need to worry about anything else.

Till soon.

Harry

PS: Want to jabber about this email? Better still, do you want to correct my sentence fragments and see how I like it? If so, pop over to Townhouse and we'll argue it out there.

Oh yes, and the reason why I keep trying to push y'all over to Townhouse is that it's a free community for writers; that is, for people like you. You can share critiques of each other's work (respectfully, of course). You can ask questions about the industry. You can talk with people who care about the same things as you do. The whole thing is free as the wind and I'd love you to join.

PPS: There is no PPS today. We're all out of stock.

PPPS: Hate writing? Love tweed? Just climbed out of a freezer? Then unsubscribe now. You don't even know what an email is.

Editor's note:

Our brilliant copyeditor, Karen Atkinson, does not wear tweed or live in a freezer and she has this to say:

> *I would like to politely disagree. Things have changed a great deal in the past few years. Many editors are working very hard to shed this image; most modern copyeditors are vehemently opposed to misplaced prescriptivism and confine it to its proper place (certain formal contexts). Good, professional copyeditors take pride in honouring diverse author voices, and training emphasises the need not to interfere with an author's voice and style; this actually takes much more skill than altering a manuscript to conform to a fixed set of rules. Many 'rules' are actually conventions which in most cir-*

cumstances aid communication with the reader, but a good copyeditor will champion deviation from them rather than slavish adherence where that communication and the author's voice and message are better served by a more flexible approach. The author's wishes must be paramount.

I witness daily online conversations which demonstrate most modern editors' opposition to the outdated view of editors as 'guardians of language' – such highhandedness is not popular in professional circles.

She's right all over again – and the world is a sunnier place than you thought it was.

Can writers learn?

It's a big question, isn't it?

Are you just given a quotient of natural talent at birth, or can you take whatever tools you have and just improve them by hard work, time and study? Are you born a Shakespeare or a dunce, without a chance to migrate from one to t'other? Or is it all about Malcolm Gladwell's 10,000 hours of study?

These questions, obviously, matter a lot. If it's just down to natural talent, then either you have it or you don't, and that first agent rejection you received might just be code for:

YOU ARE S★★T. GIVE UP NOW.

If you're not yet published, I know for a fact that you have had that thought, or at least some close variant of it. And it's a corrosive, life-sapping destroyer of creativity.

Good creativity needs a kind of boldness. A willingness to find and release that handbrake. Not just release it, ideally, but unbolt it. You want to tear the damn thing out of the vehicle completely, so you can go freewheeling down the highways of your mind, in pursuit of the spark that got you driving in the first place.

So here's the answer.

Yes, talent matters. Of course it does.

You also, I think, need to be able to construct a simple sentence without falling flat on your face. That sounds like a pretty simple hurdle to overcome, and it is, but there are nevertheless writers who struggle at that level, in which case (mostly, not always) publication is likely to elude them.

So: yes, talent makes a difference. And yes, you have to be able to handle the tools of your trade without poking a chisel through your foot.

But after that? Here's what matters:

Passion.

If you don't have passion, you'll never write a book. You probably won't even complete your first manuscript, but if you do, you won't have what it takes to do everything else. Re-work and re-edit it. Scrap some part of the original idea and replace it with something better. Get critical feedback and respond to it constructively. Get your first rejection letters and think, 'Screw you' and 'We go again.'

Passion is essential. More important than talent. I've seen people succeed without much innate talent, but I'm honestly not sure I've ever seen anyone succeed without passion.

Self-editing cojones

So yes, passion – but that passion needs to manifest in the right way. At Jericho Writers, we see a ton of manuscripts sent into us for editorial feedback. I don't do that editorial work myself anymore, but when I did, I can tell you that THE most frustrating manuscripts to receive were the ones from capable but recalcitrant writers.

So we might get a manuscript that was really quite good. I'd write a report that said, in effect, 'Yes, this is really quite good. But there are the following general problems (A, B, C, D, ...) and here are some examples of where those problems are impacting your work: blah-blah, yadda, yadda.'

Then, the writer might send in the manuscript for a second read, and I'd get it, excited, thinking I might have something marketable in my hands. Only then, I'd read the damn thing, and I'd be genuinely puzzled. Was this the manuscript I'd already read? Had the writer, inadvertently, sent me the #1 version not the #2 one? I'd check in detail and would find that where I had explicitly mentioned an example of some manuscript problem, page number and all, there was in fact some amendment, normally positive, to that page. Everywhere else though, I'd find no changes at all, or nearly none. In effect, though the manuscript needed to travel just a few further yards to hit the finishing line, this whole editorial process had advanced it by a few quarter-inches.

Those clients, as far as I can recall, have never ever gone on to get published. (They're often the ones who get most angry with us too. 'I thought you told me this was close to marketable!' Well, yes, buddy, but ...)

So editing matters. Being brutal with yourself and your text matters. An absolute desire for perfection, as near as you can get to it in this fallen world – that matters.

Keeping-going-ish-ness

(Yeah, OK, the English language probably has a word for that, and I quite likely know what it is. But to hell with pedantry. My handbrake is lying somewhere in the dirt ten miles behind me, and I have the winds of freedom in my hair. So ya-boo.)

I could give a zillion examples of this, but the one that sticks is this:

One of our editorial clients came to us with a draft manuscript. I remember reading some of it – the first draft of his first book – and I thought, nope, this guy doesn't have what it takes. But that guy's keeping-going-ish-ness was as strong as I'd ever seen. His first book, all three drafts of it, was a training exercise. He got serious with book #2. And blow me, two or three drafts into book #3, he absolutely nailed it. Got himself an agent. Got published.

And he proved me wrong. His raw, intuitive talent just wasn't that high on the scale, but his everything else was set to max.

I was going to leave my list of things that matter to just three, except I realise I have to add one more:

Your idea

A competently executed book with a mediocre idea will never sell. It won't sell to a trad publisher. It won't sell as a self-published book, or not really.

You can amp that up a bit. If you write really quite well, but have a mediocre idea, it most likely won't do anything.

I was lucky with my first book. Yes, my writing back then had a certain bright competence, but I was still quite immature as a writer. That first idea, though? Was golden. That idea vaulted me straight through onto the high ground of commercial publishing.

Dan Brown? Not a great writer, even by the not-too-taxing standards of commercial thriller writers. But his idea, the Da Vinci one, was a gloriously rich one for his target audience.

Stieg Larsson? A competent enough writer, but one who needed to shrink his voluminous, baggy prose by 25%. A writer who wasn't taken on by any of the big UK publishers because of that volume, that bagginess. But the brilliance of his idea, plus Quercus's marketing cleverness, turned his work into the sales sensation of his era.

And so on.

Ideas matter. They matter profoundly. (And it is, by the way, very common for your first novel, the one you're slaving over so hard right now, to be your learning novel. The one where you acquire the technique, learn the graft, complete your ink-spattered apprenticeship. Then when you figure out that book #1 isn't going anywhere, you toss it aside and write the big one. The one with the big, ambitious idea, confidently and energetically executed. That's the book that sells.)

That's it from me. I'm off to take the car into the garage. Apparently, it's illegal to drive without a functioning handbrake. Oh well.

Till soon.

Harry

PS: Let's talk. Get thee over to Jericho Townhouse. We shall drink fine wines and talk about the days of yore.

PPS: 'Perseverance.'

Yep, dang it. Knew there'd be a word for it. Pretty one, too.

PPPS: Hate writing? Want to poke a chisel into your foot? Got to bolt that handbrake into your motor? Either way, unsubscribe. These emails won't help you.

The wriggle of life

An editorial colleague of mine here at Jericho Writers likes to tell writers that their first job as a novelist – literally the first thing their narrative needs to accomplish – is to get readers into the story. Before your story train even starts to chuff out of the station, you need your readers on board, hats off, gloves folded, sandwiches at the ready.

And that act of engagement by the reader requires one thing above all from you. It requires you to foster belief in your world and belief in your characters. Yes, if there's a tickle of story-excitement too, that's really great, but the tickle is the second thing, not the first.

Your first job is to engender that belief: to create the shimmering surface of life.

Knowing that, some writers make the wrong call. Here are three classic ways it can go wrong:

The Error Impatient
With this one, writers get worried that they need to reveal character emphatically and early. It's as though they're thinking, 'I need to establish Character X

briskly and decisively, so readers know who they're dealing with.'

The result: they bustle off to the Emporium of Cliché, credit card in hand. The salespeople there know their customers very well. 'Suave superspy, sir? Of course. Attractive to the women? A perfect shot? Excellent suits? Knows his wine? Of course, madam. May I also offer you a chiselled jaw? A piercing gaze? We're giving away two free super-cars with every spy, sir, so this would be an excellent moment to make your purchase.'

And the result of that ill-advised spending spree: readers aren't engaged. Yes, they 'get' the character you have so swiftly constructed, but they're not really interested. Their view is from a distance. They are all ready to walk away.

The Error Accurate

Some writers therefore choose to glue themselves close to a recognisable reality. A woman like you. A musical reference to some currently fashionable artist. Maybe a brand mention, but almost certainly something to do with clothing. A familiar setting (a bedroom usually, or a late-for-work thing, or a minor work problem). And all this conveyed in language that's not quite conversational, exactly, but diary-type language anyway: the way you might talk to yourself about all these ordinary things.

And yes, OK, I'd probably prefer to encounter the everyman/everywoman character than the suave superspy one, but honestly? I don't want to read about either. The Error Accurate ends up delivering someone perfectly believable, but just not intriguing. You want me to get on board your damn story train, but I think I might just linger here on the platform and see what else chuffs into view.

Sorry.

The Error of Baroque Emotion

'Aha,' you say. 'O-ho,' you mutter. 'We know what readers want from their stories. They want to feel emotion. They want to be plunged into situations that shock, that stimulate, that shine brighter than the ordinary world outside.'

So we have gasps of agony right there on the first page. Or crashing sobs of grief. Or some improbable level of panic over some ordinary life accident (a missed train, a forgotten report).

It's as though the writer is thinking, 'Look, if I send my train into that station with a brass band on board – and a pair of performing monkeys – and a troop of dancers complete with a tiny acrobat from Java, people will just have to get on board. It'll be the most amazing train in the station.'

Well, kinda. And look: I love tiny Javanese acrobats as much as the next man. But this is all too much, too soon. The danger – the great and serious danger – is that your emotion seems unjustified. Premature. Deterring the very engagement you were seeking.

The Approach Simple

And look, for some reason, I don't know why, my books tend to open in a somewhat low-key way. I don't say that your book has to do the same. Plenty of terrific books do open with a splash of bright colour right there on page one. But they don't have to.

Here's an example of one of my openings that almost boasts about its own drabness:

Jane's driving. Jane Alexander.

The traffic is snarled because of some incident ahead. A weak sun moves in and out of cloud. On our left, a garage promises 'Probably the Lowest Prices in the Vale'.

The garage has thirty cars lined up behind metal railings. A man walking among them, talking into a phone. On our side of the railings, an elderly woman in a grey skirt and dark raincoat peers in at the cars, then over at the railway station. She checks her watch, pats her hair, walks forward, stops.

I stare at her. Jane stares at the road.

A nothing day.

Nothing has happened. Nothing seems on the brink of happening. There's no dramatic incident. No superspy, no gunshot. No burr of emotion. No desperate attempt to make the world of my story reflect the world of my reader. There's just not a lot going on.

But –

Is that enough for you to read on? Do you feel ready to step forward into my story train? I think you do. And if so, here are the components that are keeping you engaged:

There is, immediately, some sense of the physical world. A road. Traffic. A weak sun. A low-rent garage. Railings.

There is, immediately, a recognisable human character – the elderly woman in a grey skirt. She's clearly a little muddled, or a little something, but nothing extravagant. She's not a superspy. She's not someone-just-like-you. She's not someone in the grip of wild emotion. She just seems – real. And that little hint of muddle or confusion in her behaviour lends a tiny dot of intrigue to the picture so far.

The first-person protagonist, Fiona, is in relationship with something: her driving buddy, Jane. There's terribly little going on there – *I stare at her. Jane stares at the road. A nothing day.* – but even that tiny description opens up a question. Why is Jane not engaging with Fiona's look? Is it just because she's driving? Or is there an atmosphere inside the car? Why is Fiona actually staring at Jane? Those are, I agree, very little things, but we all know that stories can start out small.

To form those three points into a bit of a checklist, we want:

- A physical **setting**.
- A credible **character**.

- Some sense of the **viewpoint character in relationship** with someone (or something – the viewpoint character might be alone, but she still needs to be bouncing off something in her physical or mental space).

And those are small asks, please note. They demand the wriggle of life, and not much more. Remember that people have come into the station *in order* to board your train. To entice them to make that little further act of commitment, you just need to show that you are properly in charge of your materials: your world, your characters, the glimmer of story.

And that's enough. You can go bigger if you want to, but you really don't have to.

That's it from me for this week. You won't get an email from me this time next week, cos it's our Festival of Writing and (a) either you are coming and you are very happy about it, or (b) you aren't and you are inconsolably sad. If (b) – well, phooey and fiddlesticks. I did ask you to come. We'll speak again in a fortnight.

Till then.

Harry

PS: Want to talk about this email? Get thee over to Jericho Townhouse. We shall wait on a country platform, sit on an old leather trunk and dream about eating a small ginger biscuit.

PPS: This PS is currently vacant. You are welcome to build a temporary structure here or (better still) plant vegetables.

PPPS: Hate writing? Just discovered a tiny Javanese acrobat in an antique leather trunk? In which case, unsubscribe, amigo. These emails cannot compete.

The head in the bag

Twas the Festival of Writing last weekend, with a hey and ho and a hey nonny.

My highlights? Everything, really. It's just like a great big bale of fun and passion and intensity squished down into a weekend-sized pellet and washed down with a bottle of wine. (Or two, if you write crime thrillers. Or three, if you're an agent.) If you came, then it was lovely to see you. If you didn't, pshaw! Come next year, and we can be friends anyway.

I'll probably have a few Festival-related missives to send, but I'll start with the one about the head in the bag.

First, though:

I'm offering to run a free webinar or two on absolutely anything you fancy. Something about writing. Or getting published. Or self-pubbing. Whatever you want. Just tell me what you'd like to know more about, and we'll get something sorted.

Right. Nuff on that.

Back to heads in bags.

I was giving a workshop on how to build a crime novel, using my own *This Thing of Darkness* as an exemplar. The basic thrust of the class was how to build your novel up, bone by bone, and how you don't always begin that process from the most logical starting point. In my TToD, for example, I knew I wanted a denouement at sea – Fiona Griffiths on a fishing trawler in a storm – but that's all I knew. I didn't know the crime. I didn't know anything about the solution. I didn't have anything else really nailed down.

And then: I built from there. I hauled my big structural milestones into place until I was confident I had a layout that could sustain a crime novel. (The twist in that little tale of triumph? Simply that at one point I had a 130,000-word novel that felt long and boring. Whoops. I talked a bit about how I solved that issue too.)

But then I threw the crime-novel problem over to the class. I wanted us to build a novel then and there, to get some sense of what could and couldn't work.

To start with, I asked for an opening crime to launch our novel. One person suggested a dead student. Apparent suicide. Whisky and pill bottle. Yadda, yadda.

Now that's a perfectly fine opening thought. And, to be clear, this was suggested ad lib, on the basis of precisely zero planning. The student setting was suggested by our own university surroundings. And, OK, we all know books that start much like that.

But?

There's *nothing* there to suggest an angle. Nothing unique. Nothing pressing. Nothing to make an agent (or an editor or a supermarket book browser) say, 'Oh wow. Want to know more.'

Now that *can* be OK. My first Fiona Griffiths novel had a crime so boring I can hardly remember it myself. (People trafficking. A couple of people bumped off as possible informers. All very 1.01 in terms of crime.)

But that first book of mine had something extravagantly memorable – it just wasn't the crime. It had to do with Fiona herself; her past, her illness, her family background. And that's fine. You need one golden line for an elevator pitch. That's all. The element you care to emphasise can be anything.

But still. Because we were building a crime novel in class, I drew attention to the basic dullness of that set-up crime. A dead student? Looks like a suicide but we all know it wasn't? I wanted to do better. And boom! I was running the class with an agent, Tom Witcomb at Blake Friedman, and he piped up with an alternative crime:

Romantic dinner for two in Paris. Young Man proposes to His Beloved.

His Beloved, tearfully, says no.

Young Man, heartbroken, walks the streets of Paris, filling the Seine with his tears.

He gathers his belongings, heads to the Gare Du Nord, and prepares for a life of loneliness and despair.

> *At the station, he's pulled aside by a guard. He's asked to open his bag. And there, blankly staring and still softly dripping, is the head of His Beloved.*

I hope you can see the *instant* improvement here. That premise is basically all set up for a book that sells to an agent, a publisher and a supermarket buyer.

Yes: a million questions remain unanswered, but the basic sell is instant, strong and memorable. You can pretty much imagine the cover already. ('He proposed. She refused. And someone killed her.' 'The must-read thriller that everyone's talking about.')

Of course, a good premise is thirty good pages, nothing more. There's a lot more to be done to complete a plausible novel. Some thoughts:

Who tells this novel? Tom W saw the Parisian detective as the central character. Personally, I think this is beautifully designed to be a proper psychological thriller with Young Man as the narrator. Done that way, the book would be a did-he/didn't-he story the whole way through, with the reader changing their minds about five times through the book.

Who did kill the Beloved? A criminal gang? Some shadow from her dark past? Probably. But the marriage proposal had to be causally linked to her death. So the Beloved would still be alive if Young Man hadn't proposed. You can't just have the death as a random accident.

Climax and denouement. For me, the Parisian setting is important, not just a throwaway starter. So the climax probably needs a Parisian, or at least a French, setting. One delegate suggested we have a battle on top of the Eiffel Tower with some bad guy being hurled to his death. That's probably a bit comedic, in all honesty, but the basic thought process is spot on.

The hard part of this book is going to be knitting together the Beloved's dark past with the head in the bag. I mean, yes, you could imagine scenarios where bad guys want to kill the Beloved. But why don't the bad guys just drop Beloved into the river? Why go to all the trouble of sticking a head into Young Man's hand luggage?

You will need to find an answer to that question that's plausible enough to carry the book. Not real, true-to-life plausible, perhaps, but something that gets you over the line. (In my *The Dead House*, I had a basic plausibility issue with my crime. I don't think the crime I dealt with has ever or would ever happen, but I probably did just enough to get away with it in fictional terms. That's all you need.)

I've talked about all this in the context of crime, but the same kind of thinking applies no matter what your genre. Some strong selling line. Some good unity of concept and tightness of execution. Lots of trial and error when it comes to developing a given starting point. And just enough plausibility to hide your extravagances.

That's plotting. That's writing. And it's hard! But it's fun.

Till soon.

Harry

PS: Want to talk about this email? Course you do. Chuff your way over to Townhouse and there we shall blather. Just check your hand luggage before you come.

PPS: You do remember I said we'd have a webinar or two on anything you fancy? Yeah, well, if you don't tell me what you'd like to talk about, then I won't know, will I? So tell me.

PPPS: Hate writing? Just opened your hand baggage and found … uh … something that really needs you to deal with it right now this minute? Then unsubscribe from these emails. They'll only distract.

Oooh, tell me more

I promised you another Festival missive – this one about how to define your elevator pitch – and here it comes.

First, though, thanks a lot for your responses to my 'What would you like to know more about?' email. I'm going to go away and prepare some webinars for y'all. I'll aim to start delivering those in November. They'll be completely free. Doesn't matter if you don't really know what a webinar is or how they work. They're spectacularly easy – it's basically me talking to you live online. And if you miss the live version, you can always watch the replay. More on all that a bit nearer the time.

Right. So. Elevator pitches.

This was something we dealt with in one of my Festival workshops, and I wanted to pick it up again now. The issue is first finding the pitch that sparks interest in your book, then figuring out what to do once you have a pitch you love.

But let's start with a sample elevator pitch. This one, for example:

A. Boy with magical powers plays a key part in the battle of good against evil.

What do you think? Do you like it? Do you want to read that book?

And look: the pitch is sort of okaaaay, isn't it? But OK in a way which means that the book is basically not saleable. It's just too like every other kids' fantasy book out there. There's nothing to distinguish this book from everything else. If I were an agent, it's not a book I'd much care to represent.

So what about this?

B. Orphan goes to a school for wizards.

Or this:

C. Orphan discovers he is the son of two very powerful wizards. He goes to wizard school.

Or this:

D. Harry Potter is an orphan in the care of his uncle and aunt. Their care is very poor. Potter lives in an understairs cupboard, while his cousin is spectacularly spoiled. The non-magical (or 'muggle') uncle and aunt try to prevent Harry learning about his parents – powerful wizards – but fail. He discovers he has magical powers and is invited (via owl) to attend wizard school.

Pretty clearly, this is a series of books that could do rather well. Yet there's a way in which elevator pitch A actually delivers the best description of the books. After all, the entire series arc is encapsulated in that description. The other three elevator pitches deal with nothing more than a few chapters of book 1.

So why is that first pitch so weak? And why are the other three strong?

The simple answer is that elevator pitch B makes you want to know more. It has, instantly, that 'Oooh, tell me more' quality which marks out any good elevator pitch.

And indeed, when I do tell you more – when we jump from version B to version C – you still want to know more. Version C introduces Harry Potter's parentage. That's good, because it provides a connection between the orphan element and the wizarding one, but it introduces questions of its own. You still just want to know more.

Version D might be a reasonable answer to that 'tell me more' question, except it isn't really an elevator pitch anymore. It's too long. But you notice that even when you're dealing with something as long and detailed as D, you still have an appetite for more. (How does an owl deliver an invitation? How does Harry discover his magical powers? Why are the uncle and aunt so mean? And so on.)

These expanding descriptions of the book keep you locked into a permanent desire to know more … and if I handed you the first chunk of *HP and the Philosopher's Stone*, you'd still be burning to know how the book and the series develops. That 'tell me more' impulse keeps pushing you to know more until you've read every damn book in the series.

Which brings us back to why it's so unbelievably helpful for writers to understand their own elevator pitches. Why you need to scrap pitches that feel as bland and generic as Version A and find ones that are as sharp and precise as B or C.

The thing is, you don't ever have to use your elevator pitch with an agent, or an editor, or anyone else. There's never going to be a ten-word box that you have to fill in about your book. But you do have to understand the bit that makes readers go, 'tell me more', and then place that bit at the emotional/structural centre of your work.

So if J.K. Rowling had been working with Version A as her internal compass for the series, she might have minimised her hero's orphanhood, she might not have found key roles for his vanished parents, and she might not have placed Hogwarts at the very heart of things. She might, in fact, have produced another bland, generic and unpublishable work of children's fantasy.

But because, at least in her head, she was working with something like B or C as an elevator pitch, she placed those elements – orphan, wizarding parents, wizard school – at the very heart of the books. So yes, the series tells a story about the battle of good vs evil, but that story emerges from one founded on the exact elements that piqued the reader's interest in the first place.

The same thing is true of absolutely any decent book and decent elevator pitch. So the pitch for my Fiona Griffiths series would probably be something like this:

A crime series about a detective in recovery from Cotard's Syndrome, a genuine psychiatric condition.

With Cotard's, a sufferer believes themselves to be dead.

That doesn't tell you anything about the plots of the individual books, or the series arc, or anything else. In that sense, it's 'local', not universal. But that element of localism is essentially always true of good elevator pitches. Compare the universal-but-bland Harry Potter pitch A, against the local-and-interesting pitches B or C.

And books are founded on the local. The universal can and should spring out of the local, but the local has to take precedence. So the whole architecture of Hogwarts/the Dursleys/muggle world vs wizarding world forms the foundations for the grand, universal story that lies on top.

Likewise, the whole complex series arc of the Fiona Griffiths series is built on Fiona herself. Her illness. Her recovery. Her strange sisterhood with the dead. My German publishers, in fact, have essentially the same cover for every book they've released. Each book has 'FIONA' in huge text front and centre across the cover. The actual title looks secondary in comparison. That's an almost literal picture of how the series is built. Hogwarts, and all that pertains to it, has a similar centrality in the Harry Potter books.

So find your foundation. Find the thing that makes readers want to know more. Then place that thing, that vibration of interest, at the very heart of what follows. Make sure that as you start to expand the reader's circle of knowledge, the new elements you introduce keep the reader's interest.

That, in a nutshell, is how you write and sell books.

Till soon.

Harry

PS: Want to talk about this email? Course you do. Tie a message to an owl. Or (boring!) nip over to Townhouse and let's compare elevator pitches.

PPS: Hate writing? Getting tired of pinning tiny notes to the feet of owls? Then unsubscribe, my friend. To-wit, to-woo.

Swooping in, pulling out

I asked y'all about webinars just recently and what y'all would like to hear about.

(And, OK, about half of you will have mostly focused on my use of y'all in that sentence, you writer-obsessives you. And true: I'm not from the American South, so my right to use that word is hardly rock solid. On the other hand, grammatical entropy since Shakespeare's day has deprived Standard British English of a distinctive you-plural – we used to have thou/you, but aside from a few grizzled Yorkshire folk, that distinction has gone the way of all flesh. So how to emphasise the plural bit of the you-plural, other than *y'all*? I've no idea. Hence y'all. If you-singular have a better idea, you can tie it to a carrier pigeon and let it fly.)

Right. Digression. Where were we? Webinars.

Yes. So you came back to me with some great ideas, and we're going to act on them. I'm going to deliver one webinar. I'm asking some of my super-experienced, super-brilliant writing buddies to deliver others. It's gonna be good. More on that in due course. But now:

Swooping in, pulling out.

We're going to talk about psychic distance. (Or narrative distance. Or, sometimes, emotional distance.)

It's one of the most important tools in the writer's armoury, and the fluid use of it adds depth and motion to your text. You may very well be using the technique perfectly without being aware of it. Or you may have an 'aha!' moment in this email that illuminates something and unlocks a whole new level of your writing.

We start with a simple definition and some examples.

Psychic distance has to do with how far your narration is from your character's innermost heart and thoughts. So:

It was the best of times, it was the worst of times.

That's Dickens commenting on eighteenth-century London, and he's swooping, god-like, over an entire city, or an entire country. He's so not-close to a character that no characters have yet appeared in the book.

But you can swoop in further:

It was the Dover Road … on a Friday night late in November.

We're getting more specific about time and place now. We haven't yet hit character, but we're getting closer. We move in again:

The sound of a horse at a gallop came fast and furiously up the hill.

Things are now completely external (still no character to focus on), but time and place has become completely precise. It's not that Dickens has given us precise co-ordinates of place and time, but whereas 'Friday night' refers to a whole reach of time, the sound of this galloping horse must be heard within one specific half-minute of that night.

We swoop in again.

A coach – the Dover mailcoach – stops. The horseman asks for a Mr Jarvis Lorry. And:

[The] *passenger showed in a moment that it was his name. The guard, the coachman, and the two other passengers eyed him distrustfully.*

We're now, as it were, face to face with our character. If that 'best of times' quotation had Dickens flying over London, we're now in a coach right next to a person. We're close enough that we see him physically acknowledging his name.

That said, our view of this character is still *external*. We're not in his head at all.

As it happens, this scene from Dickens is just an appetiser. He doesn't plunge all the way into the man's head. But he could have done. Perhaps like this:

Jarvis Lorry reached thoughtfully for the note.

The word 'thoughtfully' is somewhere between a purely external view and a genuinely internal one. Yes, we can sort of see from someone's manner whether they're thoughtful or not, but the word could equally well be used by the excellent Mr Lorry to describe himself.

He pondered a moment.

And now we're definitely in his head. No one outside the admirable Lorry knows if he's pondering or not.

As he read the missive, a slow fury crept over him.

From thought to emotion, and our sense of interiority grows greater.

The devils! Would they never leave him be?

And boom! The character has now taken over the actual narration. We're in stream-of-consciousness mode. The character's own thoughts are spilling, live and unedited, onto the page.

And that's psychic distance, the whole spectrum from hyper-remote to extremely intimate. From being actually removed from any characters at all to so up-close and personal that the character themself barges the narrator off the page.

Why this matters

I hope there's something conceptually interesting about noticing this narrative spectrum. As I say, you quite likely deploy it fluidly and without noticing it. But to notice it fully can illuminate various elements of your text.

For one thing, there's rhythm. If you operate only at one level of psychic distance, your text will have a monotonous quality, much as if you had to watch a movie with no close-ups and no panoramas.

For another, there's movement. If you want to zoom right into a character's innermost thoughts, you can. This is fiction. You can and should. But you can't just crash into them without a graduated approach. You need to shift fluidly through the gears, getting closer in on the character, step by step by step. (Just think how crashingly awkward it would be to jump from 'It was the best of times, it was the worst of times' straight to 'Jarvis Lorry reached thoughtfully for the note. The devils! Would they never leave him be?' Because the approach has been so rushed, the text is unengaging and hard to read.)

And then there's usage. When do we want to be right inside a character's head? When that character is experiencing strong, significant emotion, of course.

When do we want to be zoomed out and somewhat detached from a character? Well, when we simply want to convey important external data about the scene, of course.

When you think of it like that, it's easy enough, but put all the pieces together and you have a powerful, powerful tool at your disposal.

Because this email has run on long enough already, I'll shut up now. But because these things make more sense in context, I've pasted a chunk of one of my scenes in the PSs below. That scene has a whole graduated movement from basically external to extremely internal. It's delivered, what's more, in first-person narration, which just goes to show that the issues are conceptually identical, whether or not you have an external narrator.

That's it from me. I'm about to saddle up and head for Dover. Giddy on up!

Till soon.

Harry

PS: Want to talk about this email? Course you do. Trot over to Townhouse and let's have a natter.

PPS: Did you know that we have the multi-award-winning author, Annabel Pitcher, in a cold store, batteries softly humming, lights gently dimmed?

And what is she waiting for, oh dearly beloved? She is waiting for you. She is waiting to mentor you from your first clumsy word to your final beautifully rounded full stop. She is like your very own fairy godmother of the narrative arts and *yet you aren't currently using her*!

I am tempted to call you a bonehead or even a dimbo, but I shall restrain myself. You can read more about our mentoring service on our website. You know what you need to do.

PPPS: Hate writing? Need to gallop to Dover? Unsubscribe now and ride like the wind.

PPPPS: So here's a chunk from my forthcoming Fiona Griffiths novel. Bits in square brackets are my commentary on the whole psychic distance thing. The setting, by the way, is a secure psychiatric hospital, which is not a setting my Fiona is likely to enjoy …

The transport whirrs up the little slope.

Strange how a little knowledge alters the scene. Yesterday, with Rogers fulminating away about a rest-cure for psychos, all we saw was beauty. The sparkling sea, the scatter of buildings. [External. Loosely anchored in the past. Even the descriptions suggest something viewed from afar.]

Now, all I can see is those yellow marker stones. The panic button and the taser. Those hummocks of stamped-down turf. [Descriptions now much more specific, local.]

And suddenly – it feels real. [When you shift from far-out narrative distance to something closer in, you get that sense of enhanced reality, so Fiona is just voicing what the reader already half-feels.]

This place. It's not a rest-cure. It's a supermax prison for psychos. The pretty buildings are just window-dressing. A cloak tossed over darkness.

The float whirrs up to reception and stops.

I don't get out.

Say, 'Sorry. Sorry, I just need …'

I don't say what I need, but my heart is racing. My face and neck are slippery with sweat. I have my head down between my knees and I think I want to vomit. [We're getting even closer in now. We see the sweat on her face and neck. We feel her sickness.]

A wash of fear.

A constricting awfulness. [There's something almost panicky in her language now. Very short paragraphs and main verbs have gone AWOL.]

Mervyn Rogers thought I was the right person for this particular job. Oh, leave it to Griffiths. Sure, she'll piss a few people off and make a cock of things, but it always comes right in the end. She'll sort it out.

And he couldn't be more wrong. He's the wrongest person on earth.

The driver says, 'You all right? We've got a doctor on site if you need.'

I shake my head.

Can't talk. [Notice that she says 'Can't talk' – not 'I can't talk' or 'But I find myself unable to talk.' It's like Fiona's mounting panic is interrupting her ability even to narrate normally. Her gaspiness is making her narration gasp too.]

Wipe sweat off my forehead, but it returns instantly.

A prison for nutters. That's where I am. That's what this is. A prison for nutters with an unhealthy interest in violence. [Boom! And these are Fiona's thoughts, quoted real-time. The slightly formal, reader-aware narration with which we started has been replaced by this panicked and forceful stream of consciousness.]

My heart is a long way distant from my chest.

It is a bird taking refuge in a treetop. It is a rabbit watching its own skin fold down over its eyes.

[And so on. Obviously, you can't write like this for long without crowding the reader – being over-intense, over-intimate. So gradually the scene starts to pull back again. It ends where it started, with a nice formal narration of who does what, goes where, and says what. Psychic distance: I thank you for your services. I couldn't write without you.]

Whitna raffle wur geen and gottin wursels intae noo

My last email was about –

Well, I can't remember, because the thing that dominated your reactions afterwards was my use of *y'all*. In particular, I had people writing to me from Scotland, Northern Ireland and Australia telling me that I didn't have to raid the American South to come with a perfectly good you-plural, when I could use a perfectly good Scottish/Irish/Aussie *youse*.

And *youse* feels just right. I'm going to use it more often from now on.

But that brings us on to the matter of which version of English we should respect as authoritative.

Standard British English (SBE), because the Queen speaks it? Standard American English (SAE), because Donald Trump speaks it (kinda)? Or maybe some other kind of English, because both those Englishes have had their turn in the sun?

The answer, of course, is that it's a stupid question. No particular English is more authoritative or appropriate than another. You speak with (and write with) whatever's right for the job at hand.

Now most of you, I expect, write in SBE or SAE, and I'm sure you do that proficiently enough. But what about when you have a character who doesn't speak one of those Englishes? Perhaps that character speaks (for example) African-American Vernacular English (AAVE)? Or perhaps they're someone who speaks English, imperfectly, as a second language?

Either way, you don't necessarily want to stuff your SAE/SBE into the mouth of that character. That might show a kind of disrespect to the character and the language they speak. (Which would be stupid, not least because those other Englishes are quite often more expressive. Did you know, for example, that AAVE has a full four versions of the past tense: *I been bought it, I done buy it, I did buy it, I do buy it?* Sweet, huh? AAVE has three versions of the future too.)

So you're determined to honour the status and expressive power of those other Englishes. But how?

Let's say, for example, that you have a Yorkshireman as a character in your MS. (Yorkshire is a large and self-confident county in the North of England.) Let's say your novel is set in the London advertising world. Most of your characters don't talk Yorkshire. This particular one – we'll call him Geoffrey – does. You want to mark the way he speaks as being different; that's part of what makes him who he is. It's part of the richness of your character set.

Well, we could have our Geoffrey speak like this:

Ear all, see all, say nowt;
Eat all, sup all, pay nowt;

And if ivver tha does owt fer nowt –
Allus do it fer thissen.

(That's the 'Yorkshire motto' and translates as: Hear all, see all, say nothing. Eat all, drink all, pay nothing. And if ever you do something for nothing – always do it for yourself.)

But doesn't that look unbelievably patronising? We have our book full of London ad-world types, then in walks Geoffrey sounding like something dragged from the rougher end of one of the Brontë novels. It would be hard to have Geoffrey speak like that on the page and not somehow create the idea that he was comical, or stupid, or boorish, or ignorant.

The solution, of course, is precision. (Most things in writing are.)

Take a look at that motto again. Some of the words are exactly the same as Standard British English, but just rendered phonetically – ear for hear, *ivver* for ever. But why do that? We don't generally write phonetically. When I talk, I'll seldom pronounce the last g in going, though some English speakers would. So if you were writing a character like me in a novel, would you write *goin'* for going? Surely not.

So rule 1 is: **You don't describe accents phonetically.** Doing so just looks patronising and clumsy.

But that rams you straight into the second issue, which is: what do you do when you encounter a word (like the Yorkshire nowt) that just doesn't exist in SAE or SBE?

And the answer there is equally obvious: nowt is a perfectly legitimate word. It just happens to be a Yorkshire one, not an SAE/SBE one.

So rule 2 is: **You include non-standard words/phrases/grammar in exactly the way that your character would use them.**

So we'd rewrite our Yorkshire motto as follows:

Hear all, see all, say nowt;
Eat all, sup all, pay nowt;
And if ever tha does owt for nowt
Allus do it for thissen.

That removes the patronising phonetics but honours the separateness of Yorkshire-ese by including its words and phrases in full. You haven't lost a jot of local character. All you've lost is a metropolitan sneer towards non-SAE/SBE speakers.

If you wanted to tone this down a bit (and I would), I'd use *always* for *allus*, and maybe *yourself* for *thissen*. I'd probably swap in *you* for *tha*, just because you want to nudge the reader about a character's voice and accent. You don't need to bellow.

And –

You can have fun. I once created a character who stemmed from the Orkney Islands, off the north Coast of Scotland. Even by Scottish standards, Orkney is remote – so much so that it spoke Norn (a version of Norse, the language of the Vikings) until a couple of hundred years ago. Since then, that Norn has softened out into Orcadian, which is a sister language to Scots, which is a sister language to English.

But –

It's a strange and beautiful thing. The language is sort of comprehensible to a regular English speaker, but only just.

So on the one hand, my Orcadian character (Caff) says things like this:

'Ye'r a guid peedie lassie. Th' wurst damn cook a'm ever seen, but a guid lassie fur a' that.'

You might not know what *peedie* means (small), but the rest of it is straightforward.

On the other hand, there is also language like this:

'Thoo dohnt wahnt tae be skelp while turning,' he says, as his hands show a big wave hitting the ship side-on as it turns. *'If tha' happens, we'll hae oor bahookie in th' sky in twa shakes o' a hoor's fud.'*

And this:

'Whitna raffle wur geen and gottin wursels intae noo, eh? A right roo o' shite.'

I wouldn't say that those are totally incomprehensible – *roo o' shite* means roughly what you think it might – but you wouldn't especially want to be tested on the detail.

When writing that kind of thing, you want to dance your reader along a line of comprehension and bafflement. I reckoned that readers wouldn't know what *skelp* meant, so I added half a line of explanatory text about waves hitting ships to make it clear. But *whitna raffle, roo o' shite, bahookie in th' sky* and the rest of it – well, I just wanted to dangle those lovely, strange phrases in front of my readers' noses so that we could enjoy their Nordic, sea-green beauty without comment.

My character's reactions to this speech are much as yours or mine would be. She understood some of what she was being told, but not all of it. Her own ripples of confusion added a layer of enjoyment to the interactions.

Oh, and if you're sitting there quietly impressed by my mastery of Orcadian ... well, I did what I could using a dictionary that I bought online. Then I sent the relevant chunks of my draft to the editor of *The Orcadian* newspaper, and he was kind enough to correct my text where it needed it.

That's all from me. Youse have a good weekend.

Harry

PS: Want to talk about this email? Course you do. Sail over to Townhouse and there let us blether. Not yet a member? Then get your bahookie over there to sign up.

PPS: Did you know that we have the multi-award-winning author, Annabel Pitcher, in an underground silo somewhere in Berkshire. She is sitting atop a rocket containing forty cubic metres of liquid hydrogen and oxygen, and *she can be launched at your manuscript* in less than 150 seconds. You can read more about our rocket-fuelled mentoring service on the website. Ten, nine, eight, seven …

PPPS: Need an outstanding manuscript assessment service? Course you do: you're a writer. Writers need editors the way children need puddles, mud, sticks, stones, leaves, berries and pine cones.

PPPPS: Hate writing? Worried about being skelped? Unsubscribe now and get your bahookie out here.

What is this life if, full of care...

W.H. Davies was the kind of writer you don't get so much now. No writers' groups for him. No self-promotion on Twitter.

Born to a poor Welsh family in the late nineteenth century, he became apprenticed to a maker of picture frames. Bored and wanting adventure, he started to take casual work and travel, sailing to America in 1893.

There, he spent six years as a tramp – a hobo. He stole free rides from freight trains, took bits and bobs of casual work, begged door to door. He worked on cattle ships across the Atlantic. Occasionally he passed his winters in a series of Michigan jails (by agreement with those jailing him; they profited from the arrangement).

In 1908, in London, he heard about the Klondike Gold Rush and sailed to Canada. He jumped on board a freight train, hoping to cross the continent on it, but slipped and was caught under the wheels. He lost his foot immediately, then his leg below the knee.

He never made his fortune in a gold mine. He left his life of tramping behind him.

He returned to Europe, to London, and started to write poetry. He still had no money, and lived in hostels for the homeless, and in those places writing poetry was something to be done strictly in private. To raise the funds for his first self-published volume of verse, he had to save some cash. That meant leaving the hostel to spend six months tramping the countryside, living in barns.

In 1905, he published his work, and sold it by pushing his 200 copies through the letterboxes of wealthy literati, asking for payment if they liked it.

And –

Enough of them did.

Some high-minded journalists and other opinion-formers gradually got behind his work, and Davies gradually became a bestseller and a fixture (albeit an odd one) on the London literary scene.

He's best known now for his memoir of those years as a hobo – *The Autobiography of a Super-tramp*, a book I strongly recommend. He's also known for this:

What is this life if, full of care,
We have no time to stand and stare.

No time to stand beneath the boughs
And stare as long as sheep or cows.

No time to see, when woods we pass,
Where squirrels hide their nuts in grass.

And so on.
He's right, isn't he?

I'm signed up to some self-pub-orientated newsletters, and one of the things that I find permanently daunting about those things is the sheer damn productivity of some writers. Books, four or five of them a year. Ads on three platforms, expertly created, tested and monitored. And newsletters. And conferences. And podcasts. And – blimey.

Those guys probably work out four times weekly, arrange amazing date nights, and have everyone's Christmas presents already bought and wrapped.

I'm not like that. Nor, most likely are you. Nor do you actually have to be like that to succeed.

And yes. I'm a big believer that the activity of 'writing a book' needs to involve time spent at a laptop, hitting keys. If you don't do that, you're not a writer.

But the best ideas don't always come from screen-time. Sometimes you need to take the dogs for a walk. Or go for a swim. Or walk under green trees and watch where squirrels hide their nuts in grass.

I'd say most of my biggest ideas have come that way. Never in isolation, of course. You also have to read your research. To start mapping your ideas on paper (or screen, or post-it notes, or an assembly of well-trained labradoodles).

But still. That melting place in your brain where you are considering a problem without quite knowing that you're considering it. That place where the light comes in sideways and finds new things to illuminate?

That place is precious, and we writers should treasure it.

Davies' poem ends:

A poor life this if, full of care,
We have no time to stand and stare.

So that's the message for this week. Take your phone or laptop and hurl it, *right now*, into the nearest duckpond. Walk until you see some wild clematis or a squirrel on manoeuvres.

Think of your characters, then forget them.

Let the magic happen.

Till soon.

Harry

PS: Want to talk about this email? Course you do. Hop on a freight train over to Townhouse and let's talk the night away. (Not yet a member? Then pegleg your way over to Reception to sign up.)

PPS: Hate writing? Worried about losing your nuts? Unsubscribe from this email and *save your nuts*!

A ginger biscuit and a nice cup of tea

I got an email yesterday from a writer with a conundrum. Roughly: 'I wrote the book my heart wanted me to write and now an agent says that there isn't a market for it.'

And truthfully, I've seen variants of that basic email hundreds of times over the years. It's a desperately common predicament.

What's more, I know the feeling. When I first set out to write non-fiction, I had a great idea for a book. I'd take a look at British history through the prism of exceptionalism. All European countries have encountered plenty of plot and plague, regicide and warfare, invasion and insurrection. But in what ways was Britain's story genuinely distinctive? What really stood out as exceptional?

The answer turned out to be quite a lot. There was plenty of substance there for a book.

I started to write. It was obvious, for example, that I needed a chapter on the British navy. (Did you know that Britain once had more warships than the entire rest of the world combined?) So I wrote a long, interesting chapter on all things naval.

I made it funny. If you write these things as an amateur, you have to offer the reader something in place of years of authority. So yes, people want to learn, but they want to learn in a non-scary way and if, every page or two, they get a laugh, then so much the better.

I wrote a couple of chapters of the book and sent them out to the guy who would go on to become my agent.

He liked my idea, but he rejected the proposal.

The material I'd drafted – a passion project – simply didn't sit with the market. Yes: the market was happy with a funny book about British history. Yes: my British exceptionalism theme could work well. But the way I'd approached things was still just too serious.

In short, he said no.

Over a ginger biscuit and a nice cup of tea, he explained to me why I was wrong. What I needed to do instead. What the market was after.

Now, if I'd persisted with my original plan, I'm pretty sure I'd have found some other agent to take me on. I'd probably have found a publisher, of some sort, at some price.

But –

In competitions between your heart and the market, you have to let the market win. Every time. I had the wisdom, back then, to listen to the guy-who-is-now-my-agent, and I went on revising that proposal until he was happy.

Instead of a 100,000-word+ book with chapters of 10,000 words, I ended up with a 70,000-word book with chapters of 2-3,000 words.

The advance I received, as part of a two-book deal, was £175,000, or about $230,000. I'd guess that advance was well over ten times what I'd have got if I stuck to my original plan.

And that sounds like a sell-out, a lucrative sell-out.

But here's the thing.

The book got better.

The book that went on to be published was better than the book I'd started writing. It was funnier. More engaging. More persuasive. Covered more material. Was more memorable.

By engaging seriously with feedback about the market, I made that book better – and it put a lot more money in my pocket.

Of the novels I've written, I can think of three that went through some serious editing between the first draft-for-a-publisher and the book that went to print.

The first of those turned from a pile of steaming garden-fertiliser to an adequately good book.

The second one turned from a baggy story to a taut one.

The third one dropped its bonkers-but-entertaining ending in favour of one that precisely married up with the story that had gone before.

Every time, Mr Market won. Every time, the book got better.

That sounds like it shouldn't be the case: surely your artistic soul trumps grubby materialism. Except that the market is, in effect, the body that figures out what most pleases readers. It does that in a way that's deeply sensitive to genre (so, literary authors need to bow to a different god than crime writers, for example.) And the market also knows everything about every book that has been published. It churns through all that data and pops out its answers.

If the market tells you, loud and clear, that your book isn't yet working, that is almost certainly an indicator that your book needs tweaking. Or major surgery. Or, just possibly, a lethal injection.

I don't say that the market is going to be right about every book ever written. The market will never quite know what to make of books that really burst boundaries. And there's always an exemption for genius. Those guys get to set their own rules.

But mostly? Books get better under the discipline of the market. It's happened for me, every single time. Chances are, it'll happen for you too.

Till soon.

Harry

PS: Let's have a damn good chat. Tootle over to Townhouse and let's set to.

Not yet a member? Then bounce over here to sign up. Townhouse is freer than a free thing on Discount Day, and it's sweeter than a pile of sugar with a candy straw.

PPS: Hate writing? Want to crochet yourself a life-size model of HMS Victory? Then unsubscribe now and buy yourself a really big crochet hook.

Roasted chestnuts and a glass of mulled cider

My favourite thing?

Well, I have a lot of favourite things, but my favourite for today is when you guys ask super-brilliant questions that make me think ... and generate the meat for a cracking email.

And this week, honours are taken by Nigel S, who wrote to say:

Hello Harry,

Can I ask you about warmth in writing?

I have probably read on average two books per week for the last sixty years. (That probably tells you everything you need to know about me.)

Warmth in a story has always fascinated me, and I strive for it in all my jottings. For instance, Stuart MacBride and Harry Bingham have it in spades (Lord, I hate a smoke-blower, don't you?) while M_____ and L_____ don't.

Anyway, try as I might to apply my mighty intellect to it, I can't identify what it is that does the trick.

> *So I'd be very grateful if you could give me and the writing world in general your take on why I can read a book about Laz and Roberta in a day, whereas it might take a week's stay in Three Pines to get the juice.*

And that's an interesting question, right? I'm certain, for example, that J.K. Rowling's massive success relies in very large part on her wit and warmth. So yes, you come to her books for the boy wizard and Voldemort and all that. But you stay because of that sense of human generosity at the heart. The warm blanket and the just-right mug of cocoa.

Same thing with Stieg Larsson, in a way. If you describe the Lisbeth Salander character – Asperger's, violent, spiky, tattoos, motorbike, abuse survivor, computer geek – you expect someone who is impressive, maybe, but not someone you want to spend a ton of time with. Yet the books themselves do have a sense of warmth at their heart – warmth, not bleakness – and the result is that readers commit to a series, despite its multiple flaws.

So, if warmth is a Good Thing, how do you build it? How do you make it happen on the page?

The honest answer would be: I'm not sure. This email doesn't offer a properly developed explanation. It offers some first thoughts in response to an interesting question.

But I'll start by saying that this question particularly chimes with me, because a few years back I was developing my Fiona Griffiths crime series. On the drawing board I had a character and book who seemed deeply unlikable, with a theme that seemed dark to the point of a cemetery midnight:

- Fiona used to think she was dead.
- She deals in homicide.
- The crime at the heart of book #1 was ugly (human/sex trafficking).
- Fiona's dad is a crook.
- She has no romantic attachments and no historically successful relationship.
- At one point in the book, Fiona sleeps in a mortuary. She's not accidentally locked in. She's not looking for clues. She just wants to sleep next to dead people.

A book like that might or might not be impressive. But is it something you'd want to read? Is that a character you'd want to return to? Based on that chilly outline, I'd have to say no. (And some publishers did say no, by the way, for that exact reason. The tone of the rejections was roughly: 'Wow! We love what you've done, but we don't think readers could resonate with this theme.' In other words: we're clever, insightful readers and we love your book, but we think that the unwashed rabble out there wouldn't have our excellent good sense. I don't need to tell you what I think of that attitude.)

But for the future of my career, the answer absolutely had to be yes. Yes, readers had to love the book and bond to the character. Everything depended on that.

One answer was humour (a tool that J.K. Rowling used a lot, and Stieg Larsson not at all). But it's an easy win. If a book makes the reader laugh, that little splash of sunshine will do a lot.

Another answer, and a really important one for me, is close family relationships. For all Fiona's mental chaos, and for all the darkness in her head, *she loves her family*. And they love her. Not in some happy-clappy, Thanksgiving TV kind of way. Just in an ordinary family way. Ordinary like this, for example:

> *We* [i.e.: Fiona, her mother and sister] *eat ham, carrots and boiled potatoes, and watch a TV chef telling us how to bake sea bream in the Spanish fashion.*
>
> *Ant has homework that she wants help with, so I go upstairs with her. The homework in question takes about fifteen minutes. Ant waits for me to give her the answers, then writes what I tell her to.*

That snippet shows functional, happy, ordinary relationships. And when Fiona's life is placed under stress by the events of the story, she ends up calling on her family for emotional and practical help, and the family gives it, generously, without fuss.

That fictional act – placing someone at the heart of a web of loving relationships – somehow snakes outwards from the book and envelops the reader too. The family route works mostly strongly and easily, but your story may not accommodate it. (Harry Potter and Lisbeth Salander, are both in effect orphans, after all.) In such cases, you can build a kind of surrogate family. Ron and Hermione in one instance. Mikael Blomkvist and the Millennium team in the other. It's the loving warmth thrown out by those relationships that steps in where a family would most naturally be.

But I think my third answer probably runs deepest. It's this:

Chilliness in a book starts in the heart of your main character.

And what matters here isn't your character's situation, or her achievement of love, or the existence of close ties. It's what she wants. It's what she strives to attain.

So, yes, my Fiona had difficulty recognising her own emotions. She had never had a proper boyfriend/girlfriend relationship. She kept on making a mess of the relationship that is burgeoning under her nose. Here's an example:

The restaurant he's [David Brydon, the prospective boyfriend] *chosen is only a few minutes away ... but he walks half a step ahead of me, moving a bit faster than I can manage, and he has his chest thrown out and his shoulders pulled back as though he's a soldier bracing himself for combat. I realise that this is his way of preparing for an all-out assault on Fortress Fi, and I'm touched, though I would slightly prefer it if potential suitors didn't regard a date with me as akin to entering combat.*

It's possible that I was prickly with him in the wine bar. I sometimes am without knowing it, my habitual default position. Not good when it comes to flaunting those feminine charms.

I determine to do better.

And she does indeed try her very hardest to do better. It's a clunky, awkward attempt to do better, but it's genuine. Not just genuine, in fact. It's heartfelt. This is someone urgently wanting human connection. Here's an example:

I smile at him when we're sitting and tell him again that this is lovely. I even go as far as being coaxed into ordering a glass of white wine. I realise that I'm operating as though following instructions from some kind of dating manual, but I've found out that that's usually OK with people. It's only me who feels weird.

From that point on, things go much better.

And, as it happens, it works. She gets her man. She creates and sustains her first proper romantic relationship.

But it didn't have to. What mattered wasn't the achievement of romantic completion, but the desire to find it. And indeed, as the series progressed, readers discovered that the path of true love never did run smooth (and certainly not when you have a series to write and an authorial income to generate).

And there it is. Great question from Nigel. Three answers: humour, family, and the desire for human connection. Because, as I say, these are opening thoughts, I'll be interested in your reflections. Let's all hop over to Townhouse and have a group cuddle.

Till soon.

Harry

PS: Group cuddle-'n'-chat on Townhouse. Not yet a member? Then sign up, you bonehead. Townhouse is like mulled cider for writers. Plus it's free, non-alcoholic and won't talk to you about Brexit.

PPS: Also, I should probably tell you about our Amazing Bursary Scheme. So here goes:

'We have an Amazing Bursary Scheme.'

(Blimey, I'm good.)

[Editor's note: The Bursary Scheme is an evergreen programme that runs all year. If you think you are an under-represented writer, then do please check it out. We've added a link towards the back of this edition.]

PPPS: Hate writing? Trying to roast your cider and mull your chestnuts? Unsubscribe right now, please. We don't need your sort.

The oldest book in the world

This week: a jump into the past that returns us to an eerily modern place. You'll see what I mean a little later.

But first, let's play, 'Who's the oldest?'

The oldest surviving book in the world is, probably, the *Codex Sinaiticus*. The word 'codex' means 'book': that is, it calls attention to the specific physical structure, involving binding on one side only of a set of loose leaves. The 'Sinaiticus' bit just refers to the book's location, in the Sinai Peninsula.

This codex is approximately square. The text is handwritten. And it's *huge*. The whole thing has about four million letters. It took the hides of about 360 animals, mostly calves, to make it. The book, unsurprisingly given its age and location, is a Bible. The surviving text contains an entire New Testament and most of the Old Testament as well.

But in our quest for anciency, I think we need to drop our concern with the physical structure of the document. We're looking for ancient texts, and don't really mind if that comes in the form of animal skins sewn together, or gold sheets bound together (like the

2500-year-old Pyrgi gold Tablets), or marks on stone, or impressions in clay.

Thus liberated, we can leap back further. The oldest complete text written by a named individual is the *Instructions of Ptahhotep*, first found near Karnak in Egypt. The text itself is 'only' about thirty-six to forty centuries old, but Ptahhotep himself lived in about 2400 BC, or forty-four centuries back. If you hopped onto a time machine and set it for that era, you'd hit the birth of Jesus before you were even halfway there.

The text begins thus:

> *The Governor of his City, the Vizier, Ptahhotep, said: 'O Prince, my Lord, the end of life is at hand; old age descends; feebleness comes and childishness is renewed. The old lie down in misery every day. The eyes are small; the ears are deaf. Energy is diminished, the heart has no rest ... The bones are painful; good turns into evil. All taste departs.'*

That's quite an intro, though the text itself is disappointingly bland. (*Quarrelling in place of friendship is a foolish thing*, is a fair sample of the content.)

But we're not done. We said we didn't want to get stuck on the codex as a physical structure, but nor should we get too hung up on the *completeness* of the text in question.

What we're after, really, is the oldest surviving text of any sort, and it's another set of ancient Egyptian advice which claims the prize: the *Instructions of Shuruppak*.

This text – written on a chunk of clay tablet – is about 4600 years old. And if you thought that Ptahhotep's words of wisdom were a bit dull, you'll nevertheless find them a whole class above these zingers from Shuruppak:

You should not locate your field in a road.
You should not buy a donkey that brays.

Or my favourite: *You should not abuse a ewe; otherwise you will give birth to a daughter.*

That's pretty much as ancient as we can get in terms of hard physical text, but I haven't yet told you how that ancient bit of clay begins its list of inanities. It opens like this:

In those days, in those far remote days, in those nights, in those faraway nights, in those years, in those far remote years, at that time the wise one who knew how to speak in elaborate words lived in the Land.

I promised you something eerily modern, right, and there it is. What does that opening remind you of? Maybe something like this:

Once upon a time, there was a king and a queen … (Sleeping Beauty, Grimm Brothers)

A long time ago, in a galaxy far, far away … (Star Wars, opening crawl)

Listen! We of the Spear-Danes in the days of old ... (Beowulf)

In other words, the world's oldest text starts the exact same way as a modern sci-fi blockbuster, or a poem composed by a bunch of Anglo-Saxons. That sense of a time beyond our knowledge, a land where rules could be a little different. It's like our portal into fiction.

And, given that the author of, say, *Beowulf* certainly didn't know about the way Shuruppak handled his intro, or the way the Grimm Brothers would handle theirs, you have to say that this isn't about copying. It's not a meme that went viral. What we're looking at here is something deeply embedded in the way we tell stories. Something hardwired.

I like that as a thought. Like it enough that I'd be happy to dedicate this email to that and nothing else.

And in a way, that kind of opening to a story is useless to you. Novels don't start that way. They search for the specific – something wholly exact in terms of character, time, place, situation. The deliberate murk of the 'in those far remote days' formula is pretty much anti-novel in style.

But, but, but ...

I think novels do still use that sense of a storytelling portal. It's not quite as formalised, as ritualised, but we still want to take the reader by the hand and help them to cross that threshold. We do it differently today, but that moment of transition is still jewelled, still magical. And that's a first page, or first chapter, essential – right? A little tingle of magic. You want all your reader-Dorothys to say or think, 'Toto, I've a feeling we're not in Kansas anymore.'

Succeed in that, and you're halfway to succeeding, period. You and Shuruppak, both.

Till soon.

Harry

PS: Let's have a damn good chat. Tootle over to Townhouse and let's talk. Hieroglyphs only please! Not yet a member? Then sign up, you poltroon. Townhouse is free and Townhouse is beautiful.

PPS: You want webinars? Course you do. We've got stuff planned that will curl your eyelashes and make the ends of your hair sizzle.

Think I'm going to tell you more now? Pah. Phooey. Haven't you heard of suspense?

PPPS: Hate writing? Worried about the ewe you did that thing with? Unsubscribe from this email fast, or you might get lumbered with a daughter.

PPPPS: I have two daughters.

Afterword

Why do I write these letters to writers?

Because I like writing them and because readers like getting them.

You've just finished a book of *52 Letters*, but you can get more such emails every week, and for free. Just sign up to our newsletter. It would be a pleasure to have your company.

As you'll have figured out, we always host a post-email group chat on Jericho Townhouse, our writers' community. If you need a private word of advice, you can always write to me direct.

You've probably gathered what we do at Jericho Writers, but I've put a slightly more formal explanation in the pages following. If any part of that interests you, then my colleagues and I would be happy to help.

Mostly though – thanks for reading. Anyone who ploughs all the way through a book like this is pretty serious about their writing, and it's the serious writers who are way more likely to get published. In a cool yet respectful way, I tip my hat to you. I once rode out on the same road and it's been a good one for me. I hope it brings you good things too.

Happy writing. Happy editing. And good luck with the journey.

Harry
Chipping Norton, Oxfordshire, Summer 2020

PS: *Editor's note: In his letters, Harry mentions links to formatters, editorial services, courses, blogs, and videos that you might find useful. We've added a full list of the links below for you, should you need it.*

- Sign up to Harry's mailing list AND get your free resources including the Idea Generator, Plotting Superstar worksheet, Character Builder, Self-Editing Pyramid Technique and the One-Hour Query Letter and Synopsis Builder: https://jerichowriters.com/52-letters-free-resources/
- Jericho Writers' Membership: https://members.jerichowriters.com/bazaar/full-membership/
- Jericho Writers' editing services, such as copyediting, proofreading, and manuscript assessments: https://jerichowriters.com/editors-room/
- Complete novel mentoring service: https://jerichowriters.com/complete-novel-mentoring/
- AgentMatch: https://jerichowriters.com/agentmatch/
- Townhouse: https://community.jerichowriters.com/

Jericho Writers' YouTube channel:
https://bit.ly/3fFLEQT

Self-publishing your e-book video:
https://www.youtube.com/watch?v=n1pLEjgZceQ

10 writing tips (+ 10 terrible ones) video:
https://www.youtube.com/watch?v=WlqMY5MSmsE

7 different ways to plot a novel video:
https://www.youtube.com/watch?v=vB6KcsRE98E

Publishing car crashes and how to avoid them video:
https://www.youtube.com/watch?v=02liqEjA4DI

What genre is your book? Video:
https://www.youtube.com/watch?v=SnXBl97q8lc

Article on creating a non-fiction book proposal:
https://jerichowriters.com/nonfiction-book-proposal/

Article on how to write a query letter:
https://jerichowriters.com/sample-literary-agent-query-letter/

Article on how to write a synopsis:
https://jerichowriters.com/synopsis

Article on the different types of editing:
https://jerichowriters.com/hub/types-of-editing/

Blog post on getting published: https://jerichowriters.com/hub/get-published/

C M Taylor's article on how to write a great scene: https://jerichowriters.com/how-to-write-scene/

Bursary opportunities: https://jerichowriters.com/bursary-opportunities/

Harry's *Fiona Griffiths* series https://harrybingham.com/talking-to-the-dead/

Other books from Jericho Writers

Getting Published (2020) available to purchase here: http://mybook.to/GettingPublished

Talking to Harry

If you enjoyed this book, then why not sign up to receive Harry's emails weekly? You can just sign up. You'll get an email from Harry every week and can, of course, unsubscribe at any time.

Just to make things even more appetising for you, we've put together a set of tools (plotting worksheets, character builders, a query letter tool and others) which will ease your path from here to glorious publication. Again, those tools are completely free. If you want to get them, and sign up for Harry's emails at the same time, you can just zoom over here, jerichowriters.com/52-letters-free-resources, and do what you gotta do.

About Harry Bingham

Harry is the author of a dozen novels and several works of non-fiction. He's been published all over the world, been prize long- and short-listed, had his work adapted for TV and has won global critical acclaim. Best of all: he loves writing as much as he ever did. He's also the founder and owner of Jericho Writers.

If you want to explore Harry's fiction, your best bet is to start with *Talking to the Dead*, the first book in the Fiona Griffiths series.

About Jericho Writers

If you've read this far, then you'll know that we're not just a business, we're here for every writer and we want to be there for you, too. You can join the conversation by joining our online **writers' community.** It's free. It's intelligent. It's superbly well informed. And it's extremely welcoming of people like you – that is to say, of all writers. You can find our community here: community.jerichowriters.com.

Now for the business side of things. By now you'll already have gathered something about what we at Jericho Writers have to offer. But just so you have everything in one place, we offer:

- **A membership service.** We have a whole ton of video courses, masterclasses, agent search tools, and more. Basically, once you pay your (fairly modest) membership fee, you get a whole all-you-can-eat-buffet of writerly goodness.
- **An editorial service.** Basically: we get one of our brilliant editors to read your manuscript, cover to cover, and tell you exactly where it's falling down and how to fix it. That's an awesome service, but don't go rush-

ing out to buy it yet. You'll only get good value from the service if you've written your book, worked damn hard on editing it into shape, and are then looking for help with the final stages. That's where we'll be most helpful, most value-added.

- **Courses.** And mentoring. And pretty much anything else you might require. The purpose behind all these things is to help you write better and achieve your goals for publication.
- **Events.** This is where you get to meet authors and agents and publishers and self-publishing experts and everyone else you need to make sense of your career.

If you'd like to talk to Harry, you can. Readers often reply to his weekly advice email and he aims to answer everyone who writes in.

Finally, don't think that this book is all there is. *Getting Published: how to hook an agent, get a deal and build a career you love* (2020) is available to purchase now. We'll be bringing out further titles pretty soon. They're all stuffed full of good things, and your life won't be complete until you have 'em all.

Thanks for reading – and good luck!